JUSTICE FOR SHERYL

By Donald E. Shultz & Bradley Post

TABLE OF CONTENTS

FORWARD

I was recently visiting with a younger attorney friend, Andy Hutton of Wichita, Kansas, law firm of Hutton & Hutton. He was familiar with my involvement and handling of cases involving the Dalkon Shield intrauterine contraceptive device, representing plaintiffs. He asked, "Why don't you write a book about your experiences with that litigation?" I responded that several books were written years ago concerning those cases and there might not be much interest now in the older cases. He commented, "You might be surprised," and also told me their firm and others were handling several lawsuits involving the newer Merino IUD. I had heard and read about the new IUD cases and knew that the injuries alleged were basically the same as those caused by the Dalkon Shield.

Thereafter, I began thinking about the llitigation in which I had been appointed and served as lead counsel for plaintiffs by the Honorable Franklin G. Theis, a well-known federal judge in the District of Kansas. Judge Theis was designated to handle all preliminary federal court proceedings for the Dalkon Shield product liability cases under multi-district rules. I enjoyed the honor of serving under Judge Theis continuously for about 10 years and had often thought about trying to write such a book, but never did. But I also knew that before tackling that project, I must try to finish and publish this story which my close friend, Donald Shultz of Dodge City, Kansas, and I were writing.

Don and I have tried to accurately describe and report the facts concerning the terrible injuries and tragic death of a promising young Kansas lady so wrongfully injured and killed on a dark night in September 1984. Neither Sheryl Lynn Bergeson nor her parents knew at the time that riding with Sheryl on that grim night was a huge company with a clear cut fiduciary duty to her and her family. Instead it acted as a fierce, cunning adversary determined to defeat them for its own financial gain. Truly the "like a good neighbor" company acted more "like a dark cloud."

– BRADLEY POST

About the Authors

In 1952, two young students met at Washburn University in Topeka, Kansas. They came from western Kansas and enrolled in the university's law school. After three years' preparation, they passed the bar, and became known as lawyers. Donald Shultz (Don), lead author of this book, soon moved to Dodge City and opened his own office and established a successful law practice. Bradley Post (Brad) from Meade County, lead counsel for the case described herein, worked first as an adjuster for an insurance company in western Kansas. He thereafter opened an office in Meade, Kansas, and served as county attorney for 11 years before joining a law firm in Wichita, Kansas, handling plaintiffs' personal injury cases. The authors became close friends after law school, enjoyed working and handling cases together, and were fishing buddies at every opportunity. Although usually working together, they were opponents a few times while Brad was county attorney and Don represented criminal defendants.

In Sheryl's case, Don and Brad worked closely together on all matters during all phases of the case, even though their offices were more than 150 miles apart. Every decision and strategy employed was joint. Don brought Brad into the case because he wanted it filed and tried, if necessary, in federal court in Wichita.

Fortunately for all, Gladys Hoefer, now a practicing attorney in Wichita, was their legal assistant in the preparation and handling of the case from beginning to end. Later, Don wrote a substantial portion of the book in longhand and mailed it from his office in Dodge City to Brads' in Wichita. Gladys interpreted, corrected, and typed his handwritten notes to become this manuscript. As changes or additions were made, she handled those matters to reflect their wishes and offered her own helpful thoughts and suggestions.

In addition, Alicia Post deserves and receives praise for her support in preparing this book for publication. They valued her edits, typesetting and digital file prep as well as her software expertise to help them through the publishing process, along with her graphic design skills for the cover design.

-vi

ABOUT THE BOOK TITLE

As we began writing this book, Don and I talked about what would be the right title. We thought the title would be very important to attract the interest of potential readers. We also believed it should sound interesting but be short and descriptive for a non-fiction book. We knew that Sheryl and the word "justice" should be included, but speculated that the name of the giant company involved might somehow be included, as well. We rejected that latter idea even if it might generate interest and gratefully adopted the suggestion of "Justice for Sheryl." After all, this story is all about Sheryl and seeking justice for her.

KANSAS STATE UNIVERSITY
College of Education
Commencement - May 17, 1986

GRADUATION

On May 17, 1986, 21-year-old Sheryl Lynn Bergeson eagerly walked across the Kansas State University stage in Manhattan, Kansas. She was wearing the traditional black cap and gown and received her official diploma along with a congratulatory handshake from the Dean of the College of Education. At that instant, a treasured photograph was taken that captured her beaming presence and infectious smile.

Sheryl's family was present to witness the crowning event which was celebrated with hugs, laughs, and even tears. Her father, Eldon Bergeson, describes it as "one of the proudest moments of my life," and every detail was forever sealed in the memory of her loving mother, Marearl Denning. Sheryl's younger sisters: Donnelle, Candice, and Bianca, were filled with wonder as their leader and role model received her honor. (Sister Kristen was in Wyoming and unable to attend.) Her maternal grandmother, Mary Rowland, was thrilled by yet another achievement of her oldest grandchild. "What a lovely young lady" was the unanimous sentiment.

Sheryl's First Car – Sheryl Buys Insurance?

After graduation, Sheryl Bergeson was in the market to purchase her very first new car. While visiting her grandmother in Colorado, she found a car she liked that fit her needs: a new 1986 4-door Dodge. She purchased the mandated policy of automobile insurance to protect others as well as herself in case of accident. Her parents had insured with State Farm Mutual Automobile Insurance Company, so she naturally selected that insurer.

As a result of its successful sales force and advertising campaigns, State Farm had so many policyholders that it was not uncommon for two or more policyholders anywhere in the United States to be involved in the same automobile collisions. Unfortunately, the Dilworths from Texas, as well as Sheryl from Kansas, were both insured by the "good neighbor." Neither Sheryl nor her parents had any way of knowing the self-proclaimed "neighbor" had a history of withholding material facts or choosing sides when two of its insured vehicles were involved in a wreck in order to reduce the company's potential liability and save it money.

Legally and ethically, State Farm was in a clear fiduciary relationship to Sheryl and to her heirs. That fiduciary relationship placed on State Farm the absolute duty to make a full and frank disclosure of all material facts to Sheryl. That same duty applied to her parents following Sheryl's death since legally they stood in her shoes as her beneficiaries. The "neighbor" was not entitled to secretly hire accident reconstruction experts or to withhold facts trying to stack the deck against her in favor of another of its policyholders. State Farm had the legal and ethical duty to hire adjusters and investigators for both sides and not to choose which to support based upon its potential liability and damages.

There can be no question that State Farm was well aware of its fiduciary duties and responsibilities to make full disclosure of facts to both parties. The company had been clearly told in the 1970s when it was assessed punitive damages, upheld on appeal to the Supreme Court of Alabama, in the case of State Farm Mutual Automobile Insurance Co. v. Ling, 348 So.2d 472 (Alabama 1977).

In the Ling case, State Farm insured both parties. It determined that one party was at fault, but deceptively led Ling to believe it was friendly and would settle his claim without the need for a lawyer or a lawsuit. Instead, as soon as the statute of limitations had run, barring Mr. Ling's claim, they denied it. The following statements from the Alabama Supreme Court's decision are instructive and made State Farm's duty to reveal material facts to all parties crystal clear for all future claims, including the Bergesons', in which it insured both vehicles.

> *Suppression of the truth.*–Suppression of a material fact, which the party is under an obligation to communicate, constitutes fraud. The obligation to communicate may arise from the confidential relations of the parties, or from the particular circumstances of the case.
>
> The applicable section of Alabama statute is declaratory of the common law. In dealings between persons standing in confidential relations, the law imposes an obligation on one party to safeguard the interests of the other party with the same fidelity with which he safeguards his own. Withholding facts, material to be known, is a breach of such legal duty, regardless of intent to deceive, and is a legal fraud. *State Farm v. Ling*, at 474.

A Night in September

Sheryl was elated as she left the Florence middle school building. She had not known what to expect or even how to prepare for an open house, but she was delighted. She was sure the kids liked her and she certainly adored them. She reflected on how the children resembled their parents and which parent each child most resembled. Because it was a new experience, her first real job as a teacher, she was at a high level of excitement.

Added to the pleasures of reflection on these social contacts were the pungent smells and flavors of the night air in a country town in the middle of Kansas. Picture the glow on her lovely young face and you have the introduction of an idyll-not to premature death!

The road from Florence to Marion, while it curved slightly to the west, appeared straight and level in the daytime. At night it took on a more threatening appearance because there were no shoulders, no escape lanes. Instead the ground fell away sharply into a wooded valley on either side over almost the entire route.

She got in her little car (it seemed so little after the damage that was visited on it). Small as it might be to others, it was her very first, her very own, and to its young driver this added to the pleasure of the night.

Sheryl began her homeward journey on the road described and, as she neared the halfway point, something huge and menacing screamed toward her in the dark night. She lacked the experience to judge that what lay below, off the highway, was far less dangerous than that which loomed in the narrow expanse of pavement left for her. The noise of the impact must have been deafening, but the sound was lost on her. The impact-so severe

-so final, tore through her little car and, inescapably, through her young body.

God is good. A part of dying grace is the shock that follows a terrible injury or trauma.

When things became quiet, a young man went to Sheryl's side, heard her breathing and moaning. She looked up, and he told her everything would be all right. She knew better, but she could not protest or pray aloud. Her prayers had to be silent, to God alone.

Hypovolemic shock, the doctor said, a high-sounding word for a death sentence passed on the innocent, without justice, done cruelly and indifferently. It would violate the constitutional definition of cruel and unusual punishment and could never be imposed on a felon. It demanded justice in some form, even the poor justice of a civil lawsuit in which a jury could listen, find the true facts, and impose some measure of money for what could not otherwise be restored.

Death of an Angel

Near midnight on Thursday, September 4, 1986, Marearl Denning (formerly Bergeson) in DeSoto, Texas, received a fateful telephone call. Somehow, she knew it was about her oldest daughter, Sheryl Lynn. Eldon Bergeson, Sheryl's father, delivered the tragic news that their baby girl, now a 22-year-old Kansas State graduate embarked on her life's goal to teach children, was dead. She was killed that dark night about 10:45 p.m. on U.S. Highway 77 while returning to her new home in Marion, Kansas, from an open house at her school in Florence. In hushed tones, filled with emotion, they discussed notifying family and faced the prospect of preparing to bury their precious Sheryl.

With the help of family and friends, Eldon and Marearl managed to lay their child in a small cemetery, Crooked Creek, near Leonardville, Kansas. One day Eldon and Marearl will lie on either side of Sheryl in the family plots they selected. After Sheryl's funeral, Eldon traveled to Cedar Point, Kansas, where Sheryl's demolished car had been towed, to retrieve letters from her fiancé and a tape thought to be in her car. Gerald Carpenter, the tow truck operator, told Eldon there were two types of people he did not like, liars and thieves, and that he thought the Dilworths were both. His words were Eldon's first knowledge that the father-and-son dirt contractors from Lake Dallas, Texas, who had elected to move their unsafe rigs in the nighttime, were blaming Sheryl for the resulting collision which took her life. Eldon relayed this information to Marearl. She called the investigating officer, Kansas Highway Patrol Trooper Kenneth Monroe of Marion, Kansas, who confirmed that indeed both Dilworths blamed Sheryl.

Sheryl Bergeson was rendered unable to speak in her own defense to the slanderous statements repeatedly made by the only two eyewitnesses, Edward Dilworth and his son Nathan Dilworth. The unhappy duty to speak for their beloved daughter concerning the true facts was, therefore, thrust upon her grieving parents. They accepted the challenge. When authorities refused to take action against the Dilworths and no charges were lodged for the wrongful death and suffering which preceded it, Eldon and Marearl stepped forward to defend Sheryl's name and to make the record clear that fabrications against her would not stand.

Eldon and Marearl personally contacted Marion County authorities and gathered information. They also sought the name of a trial lawyer to guide them in their effort. A former workers compensation judge from Great Bend, Kansas, where they had previously lived, recommended a trial lawyer who had appeared before him several times, Donald Shultz of Dodge City. After meeting with Sheryl's parents and reviewing the facts, he agreed to join in their cause. Since the case, if filed, would undoubtedly end in the United States District Court in Wichita, Kansas, Don Shultz later called on his friend and former classmate, Bradley Post, who likewise undertook their cause.

Because the self-proclaimed "Good Neighbor" (State Farm Mutual Automobile Insurance Company) insured the Dilworths and conspired in blaming Sheryl for causing her own death, her team was determined to make certain that truth and justice would prevail.

The six-year history of Sheryl's legal battle with its many twists and turns will unfold as we seek to describe the courage, patience, and steadfast support of two parents and their families who lived through that tragic night and the years which followed. Fascinating and unique legal questions were decided and upheld on appeal. The jury was guided by one of this country's greatest federal trial judges, the Honorable Frank G. Theis of Kansas. U.S. Magistrate John J. Wooley skillfully managed all pretrial and discovery proceedings.

A Mother's Notes

September 4th, 1986

I had finished reading "Lonesome Dove" that evening and went to bed feeling a bit restless. Shortly after 10:30 p.m., I felt a searing pain across my abdomen. Sitting up in bed I clutched my stomach and thought I would vomit. I felt terrified. I waited for the pain to pass. It lessened but was still there. When the phone rang, my nerves were ragged. I hoped it was someone from the office for my husband, Jim, so I let him answer. Instead, it was Eldon with the worst possible news from a parent to a parent. He didn't know how the wreck had happened, but the worst news for us was the end of Sheryl's life. A short time later I felt her presence in our bedroom. Her spirit swept into the room, full of fear, wanting help, wanting me to change it, wanting me to come to her and help. During this time, Jim was making calls, arranging flights and contacting relatives.

Jim and I flew from Dallas to Salt Lake City to pick up Kristin so she would not have to fly alone. She was finishing high school at Evanston, Wyoming, after Eldon and his wife, Donna, had moved back to Kansas. We three flew from Salt Lake City to Kansas City. Jim's brother, Frank, met us at the airport and loaned us a car. I don't know why we didn't think of renting one, but we didn't. We met Eldon, Donna, Donelle, Bianca, and Candice in Salina at Eldon's nephew's house. Kristin stayed with them. I don't remember too much of that meeting except for the gracious offers of food and drink from Mike's wife and the unearthly stillness.

I called Sheryl's landlord and arranged to meet him at her apartment in Marion to pick out clothes for her funeral. Through my connections as a realtor, I had helped Sheryl find a rental in Marion.

I finally went to bed, but I don't remember when nor do I remember sleeping. What I do remember is waking up in the grey, early morning light.

Jim and I drove to Marion and met with the landlord, who expressed volumes of sympathy. I walked woodenly into the kitchen where, on the morning of September 4, Sheryl had eaten cereal from one of the bowls I had given her. Her little apartment was lovely, decorated with many of her handmade weavings and furnishings. I walked into her closet and put my head into her clothes and breathed her sweet scent. I sat on her bed and cried, cradling a blue sweater I had given her the previous Christmas. Peach was one of her favorite colors, so we chose a skirt and sweater of those colors for her to wear.

The day was dreary–cool and rainy. We stopped at the sheriff's office and asked where the wreck had happened. They showed us on a map and gave me Sheryl's purse and briefcase. The briefcase had also been a gift from me to Sheryl the previous Christmas. It had been my first briefcase when I started working in real estate in Dallas.

We drove out from Marion to Highway 77, heading south toward Florence. Wanting to look for signs of the wreck, we stopped the car and started looking around. Eventually, I found a gouge in the pavement and the trampled area in the ditch. A few crumpled audio cassettes were on the edge of the road, and I recognized Sheryl's handwriting on them. Looking at the fenced field to the east, I saw a soft prairie pasture with its grasses gently waving in the mist. A young sheriff's officer stopped and asked if he could help. I asked if he knew about the wreck; he said he was the first one there. He was so young and so upset. He couldn't have been any older than Sheryl. I think it was at that point my numbness and sorrow shifted. Everyone, Sheryl's family and friends, would be expecting comfort, strength, and courage. My grief became secondary to their needs. Doesn't that just sound odd?

We then drove to the funeral home in Riley, Kansas, where we met my mother, my sister Carol, Eldon, Donna, Sheryl's sisters, and my cousin Phil. The process had begun of bringing the clothes, selecting the casket, waiting for the preparation of the body, then seeing the body of our daughter tenderly lying in a coffin, dead, but beautiful. I nearly broke down, but managed to turn and hold in my emotions. That was the first time the fear of totally losing control would begin a route of no return. Carol held me, and I stilled.

My recollection of seeing Sheryl in her casket for the first time is a combination of feelings, emotions, and memories which entered my mind within seconds. I remembered the days and nights when she was a baby and growing up and I wanted to hold her and tell her we loved her and that everything would be okay. I could not bear the words of her death; ah, the agony of those moments, trying to comfort one another, all of us in shock and grieving. I wanted to be strong for Sheryl and my mom. I nearly broke down again at her funeral when the last hymn was played, "Jesus Loves Me," her favorite childhood hymn from Sunday school and one we would sometimes sing together at night after her prayers.

–MAREARL DENNING

Sheryl's mother

He That Hath a Mind to Lie

It has been said that if a person intends to lie about a matter of public importance he should distance himself from others who have knowledge of the truth.

Ed Dilworth had a mind to lie. So confident was he that his lie would be believed, he ignored the fact that witnesses were near at hand. In the end, it was he himself that he placed *"at distance enough"* for he did not appear at the trial.

Just twelve days after Sheryl's cruel death, Bob Conklin for State Farm took a telephoned statement from Ed Dilworth:

As I was going south, this car came drifting towards me. . . I just got over automatically and gave room and the, uh... just almost instantly after they went by me I heard this loud crash and I looked in the rearview mirror and I saw, uh, it looked like her lights had gone . . . then I saw our pickup behind uh, make a very sharp left turn . . . I watched it come around to the right and knew there was something very serious happened.

The Dilworth trailer had swung across the center line and cut Sheryl's oncoming car in two on the driver's side. Ed described Sheryl as *"drifting over into his lane of traffic, colliding with the corner of the trailer, lodging under a wheel,"* causing the vehicles to be found later in a position which he could not invent. All the later investigations, including one by an accident reconstruction expert concealed from our knowledge by State Farm, concluded the opposite of Ed's eyewitness account.

This was only the beginning of a trail of lies and deception. He continued: *The tractor was off on the left-hand side, also. But all this, all this when I say left-hand side, everything, we were still in our lane.*

Q. *Were they both still on the southbound lane?*

A. *They were in the southbound lane, both vehicles stayed in the southbound lane. I believe that the lady, the young lady went either to sleep or was putting tapes in her cassette player.*

To support this last charge against his victim, Ed and his son spread two cassette tapes on the highway near the scene, took pictures of them and produced them as evidence of this story. None of the officers investigating the scene before Sheryl was removed ever said they saw any such tapes.

I think she actually went to sleep because there was no attempt to put on the brakes, there was no attempt to, or apparent awareness of what was going on. When she went by me her head was down and my son observed the same thing.

The son, Nathan Dilworth, however, answering these questions on the same date, responded as follows:

Q. *Right. Could you tell who was in that car as it came past you or was it too dark?*

A. *I think it was too dark but you know you can see figures and stuff.*

Q. *Uh, huh.*

A. *I'd say no, I couldn't tell clearly of what kind of person was in there.*

Q. *Or what the person was doing?*

A. *Yeah.*

Ed embellished his story later, charging his poor victim with *"trying to commit suicide,"* the unkindest of all, considering the pain this would cause her loved ones.

Not only did he carefully cast blame on Sheryl, but in describing a second collision in the darkness in which a car driven by a Mr. Laughridge struck the front of their pickup, Ed said, *"They were flagging it but they ignored the, uh, the flagging and, uh, and they claimed that he couldn't see. There was a trucker came up, and I had stopped him and he was parked, blocking the northbound lane...He acted like he was trying to ignore the people flagging him down...I overheard the women saying they had been to a Masonic meeting, and they had been drinking and she was wondering if she shouldn't call her husband to come pick them up."*

This statement was so blatantly false that the State Farm investigators didn't even bother to ask the three occupants of the Laughridge car about its truthfulness! Ed continued: *"He didn't make any attempt to stop until he was right on top. In fact he acted like he was trying to ignore the people flagging him down."*

About the flagging, Ethel Pinkston, a passenger in the Laughridge car, was asked whether anybody was directing traffic and said, *"Well, this fella said he was out there with a flashlight, but we sure couldn't see it."*

Although adjusters regularly use a list of questions appropriate to all collisions, Robert Laughridge was not asked about anyone attempting to direct or warn traffic approaching that dark scene.

Hattie Laughridge, when asked, responded exactly as Ethel Pinkson had: *"Well, this fella said he was out there with a flashlight but we sure couldn't see it."*

This "fella" happened to be a truck driver named Carmon Schoonover. He stated that there were no lights on the vehicles involved and that he flashed his flashlight at the Laughridge car but they said at the scene they did not see it.

This, of course, was just the beginning of the lies, cover up, and blame-shifting. More will be discussed in other aspects of the narrative.

State Farm

State Farm is now a group of insurance companies. The State Farm Mutual Automobile Insurance Company was first in the group, founded in 1922. By 1942, the company was the nation's largest auto insurer and boasts it has held that rank ever since, claiming to insure about "1 out of every 5 cars on the road." It is, therefore, not unusual for two or more insured vehicles to be involved in a collision and resulting lawsuit.

"State Farm" is a registered trademark and "Like a good neighbor, State Farm is there" is also registered. The auto insurance company has been able to ride its advertising slogan about being a good neighbor and being there for policyholders to huge sales and profits. No significant difference is advertised between the sales and claim departments, but there is a difference. We make no challenge to sales agents and their department acting like neighbors. We have known many agents who have decades of experience trying to sell insurance and to satisfy policyholders. These sales agents are usually limited to selling only for State Farm or companies within the group. Many are dedicated representatives, but they must stand aside when the claims department and its lawyers step in.

The department that handles all personal injury and liability claims is completely separate from the sales department. The claims department is filled with law school graduates or lawyers working as claim adjusters, claim superintendents, division claim supervisors, and other officials. Their work is to settle or "adjust" claims of policyholders, adverse parties, or anyone else who makes a claim for damages against an insurance policy of the company. Their task is to settle claims as cheaply as possible, especially third-party or adverse party claims, in order to control expense and payouts to save the company money. When personal injury claims or potential claims arise, this department may seek to control expense by encouraging injured claimants to avoid consulting their own attorneys. The goal is to minimize or deny claims and payouts when their policyholders are involved.

In addition to requiring legal training, field claim adjusters and claim personnel are required to attend State Farm claim schools to study policies and methods for controlling payouts. Written materials are supplied and reviewed covering all aspects of investigating and adjusting claims, preparing and submitting reports, and working with and guiding company trial lawyers when lawsuits are filed.

When injury, death, or other serious claims are involved, field claim adjusters and claim superintendents are immediately advised and certain standard procedures are followed. Fault and potential liability are the early and primary concern. Claim personnel are instructed and trained to carefully investigate and look for defenses and to gather any information that would be helpful in defending lawsuits. On-site investigations are made, the scene photographed, the insured and passengers interviewed, witness statements taken, law officers and investigators contacted, and available reports obtained, all in order to determine fault. If potential liability or litigation appears likely, those injured are contacted whenever possible, and written or recorded statements are taken. Detailed reports on the investigation, determination of fault, and estimates of potential damage are prepared and quickly sent to supervisors and higher officials. Strategies for handling cases are developed, and company lawyers may even be notified. Even when defense trial lawyers become involved, field claim adjusters and superintendents remain in close contact and remain active and available in the case. They maintain total control on what settlement offers will be made in third-party claims and have total control on the offers which will be made and whether cases will be settled or tried. Trial lawyers are hired by the company to defend when a potential case is not settled, but the company makes all final decisions on any payment. The company may even control what money the defense trial lawyer will spend in preparing for trial.

State Farm has developed guidebooks and written procedures to guard against excess judgments or verdicts that would exceed policy limits. Since the company may be liable if it does not exercise good faith in attempting to settle cases within its policy limits, it may use many efforts to justify a settlement posture. Its claims people may even instruct adjusters or others to place in the file self-serving statements to protect what has been stated in its files.

In most cases, the relative wealth and size of a defendant company is not relevant in actions for personal injuries or wrongful death. That may change when issues involving a company's wealth are involved. This would be true in most cases where punitive damages are allowable and sought to punish and deter wrongful conduct.

In the Campbell cases discussed hereafter, we note the specific reference to that issue in an important opinion by the Utah trial court. It noted State Farm's wealth is enormous. The evidence indicated that State Farm's surplus increased from $2.65 billion in 1977 to $25 billion in 1995. Its assets increased from $6.3 billion in 1977 to $54.75 billion in 1995, at an average increase of $4.3 million per working day in surplus, and $9.3 million per working day in assets.

In reviewing the Fortune 500 indexes of wealthy companies, we found State Farm was once ranked among the 25 wealthiest and even today is still ranked in the top 45.

We thought it would be interesting to see whether State Farm's Fire and Casualty Company would be successful in its attempt to exclude damage claims to Hurricane Katrina victims under its homeowner policies. As reported in the May 29, 2006, Newsweek issue, thousands of families who lost everything in September 2005 faced a second disaster: their insurance companies would not pay a dime, claiming that the insurance policies covered wind damage, but not water damage. State Farm has already been sued in hundreds of cases in which Katrina victims claimed they were tricked into signing forms stating their homes sustained "flood" damage, which would not be covered under their homeowner's insurance policy.

It was also interesting to see what happened when State Farm appealed the case of *Hampton v. State Farm Mut. Auto. Ins. Co.* (Jackson Co., Mo., Cir. Ct. No. 02CV211426 Dec. 14, 2005). In the Hampton case, State Farm was assessed $4 million in punitive damages for each of the two persons involved in addition to compensatory damages by the court where allegations of malicious prosecution and fraud were proven against State Farm. The adjuster had assigned that case to State Farm's "Special Investigative Unit."

Claim Handling

The use of State Farm's claim department as a money-making tool for the benefit of the company and its shareholders was nothing new in the 1970s and 1980s. The 1977 Alabama Supreme Court opinion of Ling (previously referenced) contained an early example of *"control tactics"* for claim handling that fit a company-wide pattern which had been instituted by the highest company officials, as it noted:

During his [one of State Farm's claims adjusters] testimony he stated it was the policy of State Farm to control the claimants they dealt with; that he knew the statute was *"probably going to run"*; that he had *"been reassuring and contacting Ling on a regular basis"*; that *"the very thing that he as an insurance adjuster tries to avoid is a claimant going to an attorney or filing a lawsuit"*; that *"the purpose of staying in contact with them is to get their trust and confidence so they will rely on him to settle and handle their claims"*; and that *"I suppose I had his [Ling's] confidence." State Farm Mut. Auto. Ins. Co. v. Ling,* 348 S2d 472 (Ala. 1977), at 475.

Mr. Ling then contacted an attorney and brought an action against his insurer (State Farm) for fraud, deceit, misrepresentation, and breach of fiduciary and confidential relationship in failing to inform him of the one-year statute of limitations in Alabama as to the claim against another State Farm insured.

In upholding the award of punitive damages which was thereafter assessed against State Farm, the court stated: *Our cases have uniformly held that punitive damages may be awarded in actions for fraud if there is evidence from which the jury can conclude that the fraud was malicious, oppressive, or gross. Id., at 476.* A jury in Ling's case undoubtedly concluded that the fraud was malicious, oppressive, or gross. Therefore, the award of punitive damages was justified.

No further effort was made to review cases outside the time frame of Sheryl's case, but we did note the effort of State Farm to eliminate from corporate memory and to exclude case files in which it was assessed punitive damages for bad faith.

STATE FARM'S INVESTIGATION INTO SHERYL'S CASE

In a statement taken by a State Farm adjuster 12 days after the collision, Nathan Dilworth told the following story:

I'm 22, I'll be 23 in October. I am self-employed. I work with my father and brother in a general construction company.

The scene of this accident was about 3 miles north of Florence, Kansas, on Highway 77 which is a two-lane, blacktop highway running north and south. It is rural, no houses or street lights. It was on a little hill sloping to the south.

I was driving a 1978 Ford F250 crew-cab, owned by my brother. I had a trailer, a 20 foot, three-axle, flatbed, homemade trailer. Loaded on the trailer was a 1986 Case 580E backhoe.

We had just finished a job in Marion, Kansas, and we were just transferring jobs over to Cherryvale, Kansas. We were not planning to make it to Cherryvale that evening.

We had been on the road from Marion about 15 to 20 minutes. We had stopped and ate and started on the road. I remember looking at the clock on the radio as I turned on 77; it said 9:15, somewhere around there.

I was following my Dad, about 100 feet or more behind him. He was driving a semi. We were southbound with my dimmers on. I do not know about his lights. I was driving about 45 m.p.h. I was keeping about the same speed he was. I was watching the end dump and all of a sudden I seen the end dump move over to the right. And then I started, with the pickup, moving it over when I saw the cars come past the end, I seen the car headlights coming past the end dump towards me. And then I moved over and I seen the car go by me and for an instant I thought, 'Oh, we missed,' but then I didn't realize, you know, I forgot about the trailer and then all of a sudden KA-BAMM and I flew forward with my elbows on the steering wheel and, uh, my knee hit the, uh, the turn knob for the window and then I remember the truck feeling like it was gonna tip over and I was sliding towards the left side, towards the left center. And then I turned the wheels the other way, towards, so it would lean the trailer back down. Okay, then the... it seemed like the whole truck and trailer seemed to settle down and then all of a sudden it just took off to the left. It just broke loose to the left and it just spun around, it just kept spinning around and then all of a sudden it took my front end and make kind of like a circle, just a little to twist in the tire marks and it brought me around then right before it stopped, the trailer tipped over and it pulled the ball out of the bumper at that point.

The truck and trailer separated at that point, the truck separated from the hitch but the safety chains were still fastened at that point. I remember when the truck driver came, I remember I said to him, I said, "the safety chains are still hooked up on that." You know 'cause that was one thing I was really curious about you know. And I pointed it out to him. And then there was just about 8 inches of damage done to the box, you know where the trailer was sitting sideways, it slid off the bumper and went up into the fender but the safety chains were still hooked to it. It was kind of like a V, it wasn't 90 degrees to the center line, it was a slower angle, and then when the second car hit, it hit just the front, right in front of the tire and shoved the nose, from the frame and everything over toward the passenger side.

The damage to the trailer from the first impact, this little Colt that hit, it took about 8 inches just parallel with the length of the trailer about 3 or 4 feet on the left front with the left side or driver side of the Colt. It went over the headlights and just caught the fender and took the door off and I believe there was two doors on that car–smashed that one door back into it and took one door off and moved the roof, you know where the cab hooks onto the front there with the windshield, the support arm? And put it to the back right, passenger side, moved it toward that direction. The Colt came to rest facing south, running parallel with the pavement, it was off the road on the northbound side. When I came to rest, the trailer and everything was in my lane, even when the second car came it was in my lane.

The Colt come to rest facing south, parallel with the pavement off the road on the northbound side, over on the shoulder.

I got out of the truck and seen that Dad was stopping so I ran up to the Colt and I remember yelling to the lady, "Are you all right? Are you all right?" and I was listening for any kind of noise of anything. I didn't hear anything and then I yelled to Dad and he came up and we met right about where our truck was and then we both went up there, I believe. I don't remember if he went up there with me or not, I'm not sure about that point, but I'm pretty sure he did. Then he said, 'I'm going for help.' So he ran and when he reached the truck there was another truck coming north toward the front of ours.

At this point I was still talking to the girl to see if she was all right, but I got no response. But then I started, I could hear a little breathing. Then I seen the truck driver was stopped so I ran down to him and asked him to call for help. He said, 'No, I don't have a radio.' Then I asked him if he had a light, if I could see if there was anything I could do for the, uhm, person. And then he said, 'Yeah, I have a flashlight!' So both me and him started running up there to the Colt when we noticed the headlights coming over the ridge.

The Crime and Punishment

Although civil punishment would be the only outcome, sufficient law existed and certainly sufficient evidence to justify criminal charges.

Under the law, a criminal offense must be set out in an act of the legislature, called a statute, to form the basis for charges. The statute must meet certain constitutional guidelines including clarity so that one charged could reasonably understand the nature of the conduct forming the basis for the charge.

The statute applicable to this case, part of what is called "the criminal code," set out in the Kansas Statutes Annotated, is as follows:

> K.S.A. 21-3404 reads: Involuntary manslaughter is the unintentional killing of a human being committed:
>
> (a) recklessly;
>
> (b) in the commission of, or attempt to commit, or flight from any felony, other than an inherently dangerous felony as defined in K.S.A. 21-3436 and amendments thereto, that is enacted for the protection of human life or safety or a misdemeanor that is enacted for the protection of human life or safety, including acts described in K.S.A. 8-1566, 8-1567, and 8-1568 and amendments thereto; or
>
> (c) during the commission of a lawful act in an unlawful manner.
>
> Involuntary manslaughter is a severity level 5, person felony.

Sheryl's death, while unintentional, was reckless, as the jury found in the civil trial, reckless conduct being the basis for the assessment of punitive damages in a civil matter. However, even with such a finding, the court in civil cases is unable to impose a prison sentence. Only sub-paragraph (a) applies to the situation here. The statute is logically broadened by additional paragraphs, which apply to similar situations. The concluding section, defining the offense as "a severity level 5, person felony," is included as a key to determining the possible punishment the judge imposes after a guilty finding. Under the sentencing guidelines in effect at the time, a level 5 person felony allowed for a presumptive period of imprisonment from a minimum of 122 months (10 years and 2 months) to a maximum of 136 months (11 years, 4 months). Had a guilty verdict been obtained at the time of Sheryl's death, the Dilworths would not have completed their prison terms (not allowing for any other credits) until at least November 1996 or January 1997, if given the maximum sentence.

The major difference between the finding by a jury in the civil case as against a finding of guilt in a criminal trial is that a finding of guilt in a criminal matter must be based on evidence "beyond a reasonable doubt," a quality of evidence which excludes every other reasonable hypothesis consistent with innocence. It is only speculation on our part, but the authors believe such a verdict would have been obtained rather easily, assuming a fair-minded jury, considering the super-abundance of evidence.

One sensed in discussing the case with the investigating officers their belief that criminal proceedings should have followed but, as in many situations with public officials, they were powerless to compel actions that the acting county attorney would not pursue. The senselessness of this death, the indifference of the pair, the cluster of acts of wanton neglect raged in the minds of the bereaved parents even in the depths of their grief and yet, to this day, abide as continuing irritants.

The zeal and ambition of the prosecutor was noteworthy, in this case a young, inexperienced attorney but from a well-respected family of attorneys. If there is no political advantage to be gained and no public outrage, then such injustices often occur from indifference and a failure to understand the lawless consequences of such neglect. When asked why he did not file charges, his response to Sheryl's mother was "Didn't you know? They're Mormons!" That, in his estimation, either made it unthinkable that they of such a religious bent could do such wrong or that such affiliation would make conviction by a local jury unlikely. That justice should turn upon such considerations is both a weakness and a strength of a democratic and constitutional system yet, individually, deplorable.

The question of why the grief-stricken family did not pursue, and influence at the highest possible levels, institution of criminal proceedings is more easily answered. The consuming desire for revenge in the form of criminal conviction and imprisonment is an entirely human response, but to their everlasting credit this was not the goal of Marearl and Eldon. Their more noble and rational aim was to vindicate Sheryl and to prove the true facts. Even the award of damages became secondary.

As for their attorneys, both knew that soliciting criminal charges and any effort by themselves or their clients from which a naked desire for vengeance could be inferred could seriously impair a valid claim.

In the end, the aim and focus of the trial and subsequent proceedings successfully concluded in a triumph which, though absent from the body, Sheryl doubtless witnessed with satisfaction.

ATTORNEYS EMPLOYED

On September 22, 1986, just 18 days after Sheryl's death, because they had been rebuffed by the county attorney in asking about criminal action, Eldon Bergeson, on behalf of the family, entered into a written agreement with Don Shultz, employing him as their attorney to prosecute their claims against the Dilworths.

The agreement is called a "contingent fee agreement" because payment of any attorney fee is contingent not only on a successful outcome but actually collecting any judgment for money damages. If there were no such recovery, there would be no fee.

The contract also provides that the attorney cannot settle the claims without the clients' knowledge and consent.

The agreement provided for a fee of one-third of any amounts received by settlement before suit was filed, which increased to 40 percent after a case was actually filed in court, and to 50 percent if the case was appealed to a higher court or had to be tried more than once. Any actual expenses incurred by the attorney in preparation and handling the clients' case would be paid by the clients or deducted from the amount due the clients from any recovery. Expenses included court costs, mileage, long distance telephone expense, fees paid to doctors and other professionals, the cost of airline tickets, and similar expenses experienced in this protracted litigation.

When it appeared that this case would best be filed and tried in the federal court in Wichita, Don Shultz brought on board his long-time friend and colleague, Bradley Post. Bradley's skill and uniqueness as a trial lawyer deserves this resume.

Bradley, the Trial Lawyer

The trial lawyer who prepares his case from its beginnings and stands by to hear the bailiff report, "The jury has reached a verdict," ought to be a hero to us all. One of the finest trial lawyers it has been my pleasure to know is Bradley Post, my colleague in this case, the one who sat as first chair at Sheryl's counsel table.

I met Bradley in law school. Of the two methods of teaching and learning the law, or, at least, to think objectively, as a lawyer must, our school emphasized the case method as opposed to the hornbook method. In the hornbook method, legal principles were stated without immediate reference to any real-life situation, whereas the case method studied actual court decisions and the student deduced the principles involved from the written opinions.

Bradley amazed me with his ability to read the casebook and recite the correct hornbook responses to the situations described in the cases we considered.

We did not become close friends or associates until he moved his family to Dodge City and began the private practice of law with a father-and-son partnership of Gould & Gould. This short relationship ended when he went back to his hometown of Meade, the county seat of Meade County. The law business there was dominated by an old, established firm, so to Bradley was left the job of county attorney, which provided a living along with some ability to pursue a civil practice in cases with which the dominant firm had a conflict or no interest.

In this regard let me say, had the crime against Sheryl happened in Meade County, father and son would have been charged and convicted of vehicular homicide. Bradley's credibility was such that he once convicted two brothers of forging checks when the checks, the crucial pieces evidencing the forgery, had become lost and were not introduced at their trial. Not only did he see to their conviction, but he successfully withstood their appeal to the Kansas Supreme Court.

Through another law school associate, he was invited to join a firm in Wichita, Kansas, that represented primarily plaintiffs in personal injury and allied cases. There he quickly developed the skill, experience, training, and respect of the local bar and judiciary. A climactic point in his career was being appointed lead and liaison counsel in the Dalkon Shield litigation for cases filed throughout the United States. The Dalkon Shield was an intrauterine device sold as a protection against pregnancy. Not only did it sometimes fail in this purpose, it caused thousands of young women to abort and suffer a myriad of other results, including the total loss of their child-bearing potential and even death. The judge who appointed Bradley to be lead and liaison counsel, as a mark of his respect, was our trial judge, the Honorable Frank G. Theis.

Back in Richmond, Virginia, where the A. H. Robbins company headquarters were located, as Bradley went through volumes of records the company was ordered to produce, he recognized a single document that was clear proof of the seller's guilty knowledge of the injury-causing nature of this product, which still remained on the market. In the trade, such evidence is called "the smoking gun."

Bradley achieved national prominence as a result of his role in this litigation and collected the award of $9 million-plus, just before the manufacturer of the destructive device was rescued by what many believed was a politically-rigged bankruptcy.

Through the years, whenever I had a case that I felt it would benefit my client, even though tried in Dodge City, I would engage Bradley to help me in the trial. While opportunities are limited in a country practice, our association was always rewarding. It was quite natural, then, that when Sheryl's parents contacted me and it appeared Wichita and federal court would be the likely venue,

I quickly contacted Bradley. In this way, my clients, Sheryl's parents, were assured of the best possible hope for justice and competent counsel.

Lawyers are not highly regarded by the public, and trial lawyers are especially targeted for scorn because of the nature of the warfare in which they are engaged. In the course of arguing the law to the courts or presenting evidence in a trial of the factual issues, the trial lawyer develops traits which, while necessary, are found generally offensive in other settings. For example, in the battle against other attorneys in opposing witnesses or matters of law, the trial lawyer is confrontational. A popular idiom in use is "in your face." The trial lawyer is often in someone's face, sometimes even the judge's.

The second trait he develops is a command voice. The voice that makes dogs move (or hide). His style is "ex-cathedra," official, final, unarguable: "I said it, that settles it!"

So that, thirdly, a bearing that is totally "in-charge" completes his make-up for the warfare that characterizes the trial practice.

The sweetly modulated voice that persuades favorable testimony from a dear old lady on the witness stand may turn with stormy fury on the other attorney or a hostile witness. All of this is expected and more-or-less accepted in the courtroom, but not–I should say NOT–in polite society. The attorney who forgets this and is unable to turn this off in other arenas is doomed to relational difficulties. Take church and Sunday school as an example, where the mood is supposed to be loving and gentle. The lawyer who is able to make this adjustment can be eminently successful in business, in the social scene, and in such non-confrontational areas as campaigning for public office.

–DON SHULTZ

Donald, the Lawyer, the Teacher & the Wordmaster

In trying to write a few words about Don as he has about me, I thought about his unique abilities with words and came up with "wordmaster" since it fit him like a glove. In checking my dictionary, I found no such word exists, as it is always written as two separate words, but I decided it was perfect and opted to use it anyway.

Words–their meanings, descriptions, and impact, when they are used, where and how they are used-are crucial for every communication between people, as well as their import among lawyers, judges at all levels, and members of the public. Don had this down. He was a skilled and thoughtful communicator with a unique style and had many diverse vocations in which to hone his skills. He was both an excellent student and teacher, and I consider Donald Shultz a top-notch lawyer, whether representing plaintiffs or defendants. When speaking, writing, or providing explanations, impact, clarity and interest were of vital importance to Don. He taught legal seminars and wrote countless legal briefs. He had always been a Bible scholar and taught Sunday school, and he sometimes filled in as a lay minister at his church. Sometimes we discussed word puzzles at which I thought him unrivaled. He informed me that his wife, Carolyn, was even better than he. It was my honor and pleasure to designate Don as lead author of this book for these reasons, even though he might try to deny such praise.

Although Don and I have written many hundreds of legal briefs and other documents in our professional lives, we are novices in writing a book and this will be our first. In this book we attempted to limit the use of what some refer to as "legalese" or the jargon lawyers use to discuss issues and facts. However, some is critical to accurately explain the chain of events.

Most law offices and law libraries are filled with books which contain official court opinions rendered in state and federal courts. These opinions are signed by the judge writing for the majority of the panel hearing the appeal, but may also include concurring or dissenting opinions by other judges hearing the case. (Most judges are good writers and are probably among the best in our profession.) These opinions become known as legal "precedent" for later cases which may involve the same or similar legal issues.

Near the end of this book, a single word used by the highest appellate courts to describe and measure wrongful conduct will be noted and readers will be invited to judge for themselves whether that word was applicable to the conduct exhibited against Sheryl Bergeson in this case.

–Bradley Post

"LIKE A GOOD NEIGHBOR"- TIL SHERYL GOT THERE

A lawyer's preparation for a jury trial is equaled by no other human experience. After months, often years of investigating facts, re-creating the events-usually a relatively brief episode-resulting in injury or death, then putting together the testimonial pieces in a meaningful way that appeals to normal human emotion all the while satisfying the standards of the law, challenges the ingenuity and imagination beyond belief.

Sheryl is dead. That cruel fact can not be repealed. The trial seeks some little recompense for this grievous, avoidable loss of life. We list our witnesses and a summary of what they can tell the jury, not us. We have already rehearsed the details, waking and sleeping, that will reveal the kind of person she was and the conduct and demeanor of those who, with such indifference, caused her death.

We would call first to the witness chair Sheryl's mother. Who knows more about a lovely child? Who more displays what the child would become?

Marearl Denning was born and grew up on a farm in Riley County, Kansas. She attended school there through high school, where she met Eldon Bergeson. Eldon and Marearl were married in 1963 and lived in Osage City, Kansas. Sheryl was born on July 27, 1964. They moved to Lincoln, Nebraska and Eldon was employed by Natural Gas Pipeline after he graduated from Nebraska Technical School in Milford, Nebraska. After a short time in Beatrice, Eldon was transferred to Great Bend, Kansas in 1969 where two sisters joined Sheryl: Kristin Kay, born May 20, 1969, and Donelle Jean, born August 15, 1974.

Sheryl lived out her early life during the family's stay in Great Bend, from 1969-1982. Her distinct character, talents and skills unfolded there before her pleased and proud parents.

Always an honor student and self-driven, she was not satisfied with the normal academic load but participated in organizations both in and out of school, including Girl Scouts (constantly completing merit badge demands) and youth choir at the church where she and her family were active. She developed expertise in photography. She learned sign language, played the piano, was a natural athlete, and merged her interest in sports with the faith in God she developed early, becoming an officer in the Fellowship of Christian Athletes.

In 1977 the family experienced the difficulty of divorce. Marearl went to college and agreed for the sake of the children they should remain with Eldon, whom Marearl describes yet as a fine man. Despite the rupture of their union, the couple talked often and shared decisions concerning the children.

Investigation and Discovery

One advantage of presenting claims in federal courts is the early and liberal use of discovery. "Discovery," as the name implies, covers those laws that compel the adverse party to disclose records and reveal facts within its possession. Because of its long history, federal judges and magistrates having to deal with these procedures understand and enforce discovery in the interest of making available for trial evidence which formerly was concealed.

Discovery takes several forms. As to expected testimony, hearings called "depositions" compel the testimony of adverse witnesses under oath in question-and-answer form, which is recorded verbatim by a reporter certified to reproduce questions and answers exactly and completely. The written transcript of such testimony can then be used to produce facts from an absent witness or, most frequently, to hold in check or "impeach" where necessary, the testimony of a live witness at the time of the trial. Few witnesses dare to deviate from testimony preserved in this way when a printed copy lies open before them on the witness stand. If a person wishes to deviate now from what was answered then, he or she should have a believable explanation ready.

The "request for admissions," another form of pleading, lists certain facts numerically and in writing served on the adverse party which it must answer within a specified time. Matter not denied, explained or objected to in the time allowed is deemed admitted, thus avoiding the need to produce evidence as to such facts at the trial.

A major resource in discovery is the "request for production, inspection, and copying," which allows the lawyer to look at the original records, inspect them, and copy portions he deems helpful. Lawyers may inspect not only such records as have evidentiary value, but also those which make mention of other files, facts, or persons which may lead to other usable evidence.

By careful and diligent pursuit of these, the trial attorney is able to discover all the evidence available to his client's cause. It is always the client's case, and, while the lawyer must be free to follow his instincts gained by experience, there are times when he must remember whose case it is he is trying, keep the client informed, and, in some instances, get the client's permission to proceed.

Discovery in federal court is often the topic of conferences with a federal magistrate who reviews requests, rules on objections, and may compel recalcitrant parties to comply.

Before the days of liberal discovery, trials were "by ambush" the client's case depended largely upon partisan witnesses, and great bodies of truth were successfully concealed by culpable parties, often insurance companies. The result was often no recovery of damages or inadequate damages for the injury suffered. Discovery evens the playing field and, of course, it acts both ways. Those being sued have the right to see the cards the plaintiff is holding.

When the discovery tools have been exhausted, the final step is a "pretrial conference." In a hearing or hearings before a judge, each party sets out the issues to be tried, a list of witnesses with what their testimony will cover, stipulations of facts the parties agree upon, amendments to pleadings that are needed, what the plaintiff contends, what the other party or parties contend, the theory of the claim (why plaintiff is entitled to the relief asked for), a list of the exhibits which have been identified by each party, expert witnesses and the substance of their testimony, orders of the court, sometimes the estimated time of trial, and the fact that the matter is ready for trial and the name of the judge who will preside.

One order of the court, usually the final one recorded, is that the pretrial order will control and will not be modified except by consent of all parties or order of the court.

PRETRIAL PLEADINGS

In this case there were actually two pretrial orders, each of which was signed by the attorneys and approved by the court. The first was dated November 3, 1988. After completion of scheduled discovery and careful consideration of the facts and issues, on June 28, 1989, we filed a motion to amend the pretrial order to include a claim for punitive damages. It was approved by the court's order of August 22, 1989.

By letter of January 17, 1990, the defense made a change in its contentions: 1) admitting liability for compensatory damages only for Nathan Dilworth, but denying liability for any punitive damages, and 2) continuing its denial of both compensatory and punitive damages for Edward Dilworth, the father and owner of the rigs involved. Their changes also re-listed the following contentions against Sheryl Bergeson which had been contained in the first pretrial order:

Defendants' Contentions

Defendants deny they were negligent as alleged by plaintiff. Instead, they assert that the deceased plaintiff, Sheryl Bergeson, was at fault in:

A. Driving left of center;

B. Failing to keep her vehicle under control;

C. Failing to keep a proper lookout; and

D. Failing to take evasive action.

The amended pretrial order with the above changes was filed on February 16, 1990, and trial in federal court began on April 23, 1990.

SPECIALIZATION-
THE TRIAL PRACTICE

As in the medical profession, certain areas of the law demand specialization that allows an attorney with special aptitude and interest to develop extraordinary skills for the benefit of those needful of such expertise. Examples would be in areas of taxation, taking of property for public use called "condemnation" or "eminent domain," patent and copyright, and, of course, trial practice, those who try primarily civil actions based on death and personal injury.

In such a specialized practice, the investigation of the facts and the discovery pursued are of the utmost importance.

In a perfect world, much of the investigation could be completed by a secretary ordering copies of accident reports, photographs taken at the scene, together with other public records. Legal assistants can take statements of the various witnesses and pursue other collateral matters such as negative statements of people involved who have nothing important to add but who must be prevented from surprising the attorneys with facts previously concealed. It is a real protection when a person who has given a statement saying, "I know nothing!" appears at trial and who then must explain his earlier denial. But this is not a perfect world. The lawyer must do most of the work preparing for trial.

During the investigative stage, relations with the clients must also be maintained by reports of progress and regular communication. This is a sensitive area that can be a serious distraction to the attorney. Often misunderstandings arise from "lawyer talk." One such event arose as a result of a telephone conversation with Marearl, Sheryl's mother, on October 23, 1986.

In a doleful letter Marearl wrote,

I was somewhat concerned and confused after our conversation on October 23 . . . . I think you mentioned you were finishing a federal case and would start on Sheryl's case following that. You also mentioned that just because a case may be awarded favorably, that did not mean we could collect. I understand that, but are you indicating that you have had second thoughts about this case?

What had happened in my practice that brought about this bit of warning to our clients-just because you get a verdict, it is no guarantee that you will collect the money-came about in this way. I had just gone through a case in which we achieved a verdict of $12,000 for a client, only to have the defendant file bankruptcy, thereby rendering the verdict worthless. The defendant was a franchisee from Phoenix, Arizona. They sent an attorney from Phoenix to defend in the trial and, for those reasons, I had no idea that we would be unable to collect. But I had been reprimanded by the committee on professional ethics of the bar association for failing to advise that client in advance of that possibility, so I was trying to avoid a similar result here. And, at this point, we were still unaware of the amount of the insurance State Farm provided for the Dilworths and what financial assets, if any, they might have available.

After explaining all this to Marearl, she was satisfied and received my reassurance that I had not had any such "second thoughts."

–DON SHULTZ

THE JURY PANEL

When the jury is finally selected, counsel hope to have an impartial cross-section of the community where the case is being tried. Our jury panel included 3 men and 5 women from Wichita and the surrounding area. They included an aircraft parts checker, a bank agricultural loan officer, a state agency office worker, a claims auditor for an outdoor gear manufacturer, a machinist, a computer systems analyst, a homemaker, and an aircraft assembly worker.

During the voir dire examination (the initial questions to the potential jurors) to select the jury, attorney for the defense asked,

Now, Mr. Dilworth, Edward Dilworth, is not here and he'll not be here with us this week of the trial, and Judge Theis has already told you that shouldn't enter into your considerations in deciding the case. Will you all, will all of you promise me that it will not enter into your deliberations in deciding the case?

But when the case was finally submitted to them for deliberations, this is what the court instructed them in Instruction 12:

If a party to this case has failed to offer evidence or to produce a witness within his power to produce, you may infer that the evidence or testimony of the witness would have been adverse to that party, if you believe each of the following elements:

1) The evidence or witness was under the control of the party and could have been produced by the exercise of reasonable diligence.
2) The evidence or witness was not equally available to an adverse party.
3) A reasonably prudent person under the same or similar circumstances would have offered the evidence or produced the witness if he had believed the evidence or the testimony would be favorable to him.
4) No reasonable excuse for the failure has been shown.

The Trial Proceedings

The following is taken from the transcript from the beginning of the trial. Judge Theis is speaking.

The Court: Okay, ladies and gentlemen of the jury, the next...we'll begin the trial proper now, which begins with the opening statements by the attorneys on each side. Under the rules of the federal court, each side has gone through what is called pre-trial procedures of discovery in which they have examined by deposition and questioned the witnesses on either side, so each one knows quite a bit about each other's case and what...there is not too much surprise in trials anymore. The opening statements will tell you what they expect to prove by their witnesses and evidence and documents on each side of the case. And the opening statement is sort of a table of contents or a preview of their side of the case. The closing arguments of the lawyers, they are the words of the lawyers. The plaintiff will go first on their opening statement and then the defendant will give his and then we'll get into the testimony of the plaintiff's case. They will put on their witnesses and evidence, and then after they rest and conclude their evidence, the defendant will have an opportunity to put on their evidence and their witnesses. Then there may be two more possible trial interludes, usually not, but there can be rebuttal and surrebuttal. And then the last part will be the closing arguments, and the very last part will be my instructions on the law, although I may have instructions on the law as we go along in the case, it's hard to tell. But the main instructions come last. If you are ready, Mr. Post, you may now present the plaintiff's closing argument. I mean, opening statement. Pardon me. Sometimes I read in the paper that the lawyers had presented their opening argument, and that's a misnomer, of course, but go ahead, Mr. Post.

In the opening statement, counsel for the parties involved are permitted, before any evidence is presented, to inform the jury of their respective versions of the events giving rise to litigation and the remedy each suggests should be the decision of the jury.

In this case, liability for negligence had finally been admitted by Nathan only so the only issue on this part of our claim was the amount of damages sustained by Sheryl's parents for the loss of this dear child expressed in terms of bereavement, loss of society, funeral expenses, and the economic benefits lost.

However, when our investigation was completed, the pretrial order was amended to make a claim for punitive, or what are called "exemplary damages," allowed by the law to punish the wrongdoer for conduct so egregious as to constitute gross neglect of duty, bordering on willfulness, and also to serve as a warning to others. This second claim, for punitive damages, was denied by both Dilworths. Since Nathan was the driver of the vehicle that actually collided with Sheryl's little car, it was necessary to show that Nathan and his father, Ed, were acting in concert, engaged together in a single enterprise so that the act of the one was deemed the act of both of them.

In his opening statement, Bradley began with a comment on the procedure that he would go first and Mr. Warta would follow, and that he would not try to instruct on the law since that was up to the judge.

Opening Statement

We must diverge from the main path of our history of this case to discuss the opening statement in its broader aspects.

It is widely agreed among attorneys who regularly try cases that the opening statement strongly influences the outcome. University studies of juror responses confirm this belief.

A narrative in this regard is not out of place. Bradley one day appeared as speaker in a seminar for trial lawyers in Dodge City. His topic was the opening statement. What he presented to us was material he had gleaned from *Goldstein Trial Technique*, now edited by Goldstein's successor, Fred Lane J.D., and published by West Group, a Thomson Company. Bradley had previously attended Fred Lane's week-long lectures in Chicago, covering trial practice generally but also including trials that involved medical questions.

The outline Bradley presented was so obviously on target that I began following it faithfully. Not surprisingly, I began regularly winning cases that before might have been somewhat doubtful of success. I made that outline a part of our "Black Book" in our office, which contained important items of this nature for ready reference.

Of course, reference was made in law school to opening statement and the only thing that sticks in my memory from that course was that counsel was to avoid objection, by introducing each topic by the phrase "we will show by our evidence" that such and such a thing was true. The impression that left on my young mind was that having an objection lodged to your opening statement was a fearful thing to be avoided at all costs. This destructive concept dominated my thinking until Bradley freed me from such fears and set me on the road to success. I was also later privileged to attend a week-long seminar in Wichita led by Fred Lane personally.

A skeleton outline of the points to be covered in opening statement follows. For refinements on the topic the reader is referred to *Goldstein Trial Technique*.

–DON SHULTZ

OPENING STATEMENT CONTENTS

INTRODUCTION:

• Counsel introduces himself, his clients, sometimes opposing counsel and the court (if this has not been done previously).
In the opening statement we were encouraged to state the purpose: to give the jury a birds-eye view of the entire case, which would otherwise come to them in bits and pieces, in order to provide a frame of reference.

PARTIES AND KEY WITNESSES:

• Here something is said about the clients and those who will provide important bits of testimony to underline and emphasize.

THE SCENE:

• In most collision cases this will describe the location and wherever else the events in litigation were concentrated.

THE INSTRUMENTALITY:

• What the thing was that caused the injury by failure or by contact.

PRACTICES AND PROCEDURES:

• Here we list such matters as the "rules of the road" or recognized procedures or standards of practice that are involved.
Any *deviation from applicable standards* by the adverse party should be emphasized.

WEATHER:

• Factors affecting the events whether negative, "The weather was clear and the road was dry" or affirmative, "It rained steadily so that both traction and visibility were limited."

DATE AND TIME:

CREATION OF THE ISSUES:

• What the jury may be expected to decide.

HOW IT HAPPENED:

• A "picturization" [word picture] of the important events through the eyes of the client or key witness.

FACTUAL BASIS OF LIABILITY:

• Stated to fit the applicable statute or other law which will be included in the court's instructions.

Anticipation and Refutation of Defenses:

- "They will claim, but we will show . . . "

Damages:

- The financial consequences and economic impact to the client.

Conclusion:

- "Here's what we ask you to do."

Bradley's opening statement in this case was necessarily reduced from the detail described in the preceding outline by virtue of the fact that Mr. Warta had conceded fault on the part of Nathan Dilworth even though he continued to deny responsibility for Ed Dilworth on all counts. Also, he did deny the claim for punitive damages as to both father and son.

So Bradley's opening statement covered the joint responsibility of both. Not only was the Dilworths' contract with the Corps of Engineers to be performed as partners, but they also jointly made the decision to move at night, and they both knew well the dangers their rigs offered to other users of that highway.

The joint nature of their operations needed to be covered as to the joint liability for the actual damages claimed. In addition, it was necessary to enumerate those matters of neglect and indifference and guilty knowledge of both that would form a basis for the jury to allow punitive damages that would serve to punish those defendants and to serve as a warning to others.

It was not easy to convey here the impression on the jury that an opening statement carefully prepared and delivered in the convincing style which Bradley, of all the trial attorneys I have known, possessed.

One practice in the opening statement not mentioned was to hold back, not tell the jury every damning item of evidence, but to permit the story to unfold in such a way that the jury would discover on their own some important elements of fact, which had the effect of making them even more strongly convinced of the truth of the rest of it.

Remember that all the facts reported are calculated to meet the precise requirements of the applicable law which would be given in the instructions at the end of all the testimony by the presiding judge. While some allusions are permitted in reference to the rules of the road and applicable standards as to general conduct, the lawyer is not permitted to say. "This is the law applicable to this situation." That is the judge's province, and he jealously guards it even when the opposing party does not.

At any rate, Bradley, in his delivery, is so believable in part because he carefully avoids exaggeration, but more so because of his forthright appearance. After discussing the elements outlined, the rules of the road, and the departure from them by the Dilworths, the dangerous instrumentality of the overloaded, homemade trailer with the elongated hole and stripped treads on the ball hitch, Bradley concluded with his request for damages. He asked the jury to allow only $100,000 for the bereavement and other non-economic damages, since we were prohibited by the legislature from adding that this was the limit, or "cap," placed on this element of damages. The reason for specifically requesting only the limited sum was in an effort to dissuade the jury from adding, in its zeal, an amount far in excess of the limit, which in fact they did do, resulting in a reduction in the verdict. The jury in this case did allow $250,000. As a result the award had to be reduced by the court by the $150,000 excess, money the jury would have most probably added elsewhere. Efforts to get the legislature to change this unjust restriction, which keeps secret the fact that there is a limit and how much it is, have failed up to this time. (We also believe the statute is unconstitutional because the amount is hidden and an infringement on the right to trial by jury.)

Bradley had requested punitive damages of only $250,000 but explained the issue was entirely up to the jury and that they might find that amount was not enough or too much. The jury awarded $500,000, an amount which would surely have been increased had the jury known of the limit on non-economic damages.

Bradley displayed the ball hitch at one point in his closing argument, and one of the jurors, an engineer, asked to see it. Bradley handed it to him. There was no objection to this unusual event.

Opening Statement by Mr. Warta

In his opening statement, Mr. Warta very wisely analyzed and dealt with the issues open to him for argument. Having admitted the fault of Nathan only, his only course was to discuss those matters of fact which should not be considered in assessing the damages.

He opened with a brief declaration of the difficulties in dealing with death and the rules that governed deciding claims for resulting damages. He first praised Sheryl then reminded that such sympathy should not be the basis for fixing the amounts. He then turned to the claim that Ed was not responsible for the conduct of Nathan.

From there, having made reference to Ed, he referred to his "very uncaring comments after this accident," which he explained as "a misguided effort to protect his son, Nathan." He then added that these had nothing to do with the issue of Ed's legal liability for the accident. *(Note: Defense attorneys use the term "accident" for what the plaintiff says was a "collision." The repeated use of "accident" is used to suggest diminished responsibility.)*

He then described the Dilworth family, their employment with the Corps of Engineers, and their habits of contracting and dividing the proceeds. Then, going to the events of that evening, he argued that Ed had "not contributed what so ever" to Nathan's conduct. He denied that either Ed or Nathan were aware of any problems with the trailer before the accident.

On punitive damages, he repeated that Nathan had no prior knowledge and there was no basis for an award of punitive damages.

He then discussed the brevity of Sheryl's consciousness, suggesting that she never was conscious in any real sense. (The jury nevertheless allowed her estate $100,000 for this element called "conscious pain and suffering.")

After again touching on the allowable damages, he closed.

The Order of Presentation

As in storytelling, and an additional matter to which much thought must be given, is the order in which witnesses and exhibits are put before the jury. Usually, plaintiff leads with the witnesses who can present the most complete narrative of what happened and gave rise to the claim for damages. Other evidence is produced so as to present the most powerful imagery, occasionally interrupted to accommodate a witness out of the preferred order who happens to be needed elsewhere at the time.

During this testimony, called *direct examination,* opposing counsel may object to questions that are *leading,* that is, in which the answer is supplied by the question and the witness asked to agree. A question may be compound, calling for two answers. The witness may not be competent to answer the question, having disclosed that he was not present at the time and place and could not directly know the answer (the objection is *incompetent*) unless he answers with what he has heard someone say, which raises the objection as *hearsay.* Another objection is that the answer is *irrelevant,* that is, it answers to none of the factual issues of the case. The court, of course, rules on each objection. *Overruled* means the witness is allowed to answer. *Sustained* means the witness may not answer. If he does, counsel may ask that the response be *stricken from the record and the jury instructed to disregard it,* or, if not harmful, counsel may ignore it, not wishing to add emphasis to a meaningless answer.

Cross-Examination

Each party is given the opportunity to cross-question each witness presented by any other party. This is called *cross-examination.* As the name suggests, this examination tends to "cross," or challenge, such things as the accuracy of observation, the physical or psychological influence on the ability to observe, and the influences of animosity, favor, or other prejudicial preconceptions to which we are subject. The witness may be impeached by prior inconsistent statements or other conduct inconsistent with the opinions expressed.

Consideration of benefits flowing to the witness out of relationships with the party favored by their testimony, may be very important. Benefits may even include cash payments, particularly to experts. "How much were you paid for your testimony?" will almost always draw the response, "I am not paid for my testimony. I am paid for my time," but when the amount of payment is revealed it may bring a gasp from the jury.

The object of cross-examination is to destroy or at least weaken the value of that testimony.

Witnesses are often intimidated by the threat of cross-examination. Fear often bears fruit in completely truthful responses. Witnesses that are obviously thoughtful and confident on direct examination often escape cross. There is no advantage in allowing a witness to repeat, reinforce and add to the effectiveness of their testimony. Skilled lawyers usually try to leave the impression that the testimony is of no value, responding confidently, "No questions!"

The examination and later cross-examination of Nathan Dilworth by Bradley Post amply illustrated how productive to the Bergesons such skillful use of the opportunity presents.

The Worthy Client

One thing trial lawyers learn, sooner or later: You may have a factual case that would support substantial damages and yet you fail at trial because you do not have a worthy client. Stated another way, you had a worthy case but an unworthy client, one the jury saw had other motives than justice or otherwise was considered not worth the jury's time.

Sometimes a worthy client can carry a weak legal and factual case because of the esteem developed in the course of trial.

The great advantage counsel had in presenting Sheryl's case was, in addition to clear, aggravated fault, that our clients, Eldon Bergeson and Marearl Denning, presented as honest people of integrity not motivated by greed or vengeance, seeking only just punishment for the crime, which these defendants had otherwise escaped.

In addition to the obvious demonstrable character of her parents, Sheryl herself emerged as an ideal daughter, excellent in every way, the obvious product of noble parentage and exemplary rearing.

The contrast provided in this case, in comparing the victim and her parents with the defendants Dilworth, tended to enhance still more the worthiness of Sheryl, her parents, and their claims.

Lawyers do not have the privilege of creating the image of their clients any more than they can manufacture the factual or legal basis for their cause of action. Had we possessed that power in this case, we could not have equaled the perfections entrusted to our care.

THE TRIAL

April 23, 1990, was spent in selecting the jury and opening statements of counsel, except for the reading of three exhibits which described Sheryl's injuries so graphically that her parents were asked to be excused to avoid hearing such a painful beginning of the evidence.

After these exhibits were in evidence, Judge Theis instructed the jury as follows:

The Court: Very well. We'll stand in recess, ladies and gentlemen of the jury, until 10 o'clock in the morning, and we'll continue with the evidence in the case. As new jurors, permit me to tell you some of the things that I want you to do or refrain from doing and these are known as the admonitions of the Court. You are officers of the court like I am. You are the judges of the facts in the case. I am the judge of the law, but don't talk about this case at home, at any time. I know your folks at home are curious about what you're doing, but you've got the ringside seats, and you're not to discuss it during the case. You can tell them about it later. I don't think there will be any particular news account of the case, but if there were we would ask you to refrain from reading about it. Don't get curious about anything in the case. It will be answered through evidence, I'm sure.

Sometimes, people resort to dictionaries and encyclopedias or something and then we've all wasted our time, we have a mistrial. And don't let anybody talk to you about the case, I'm sure they won't. As long as you are jurors, you have a jury room down there and witnesses may be in the hall and so forth, but the lawyers will let you alone, not because they don't like you or anything like that, but they don't want to appear to be leading to the jury or incurring any favor on the jury. So if they don't stop or chat or anything, don't expect them to do that. The same thing with any witnesses. Just keep to yourselves. Don't form any opinions or conclusions about the case until you have heard it all. You are going to hear the evidence on the plaintiff's side and on the defendant's side. You have to hear the arguments and hear the instructions of the Court. So you have no guidelines, you form impressions as you go along on the credibility of the witnesses and kind of keep it to yourself and don't make up your mind until the case is over. The place to decide the case is in the jury room, not over lunch or in the court or driving back to or from in your car. I know at least three of you are from down around Ark City or Winfield and the rest of you are from Wichita. Those are things that I would suggest very strongly that you do or not do. I won't repeat them all the time. If you do that, we'll get this trial over in due course, and it may not be pleasant like the evidence you have just heard, but as far as your job and mine, the lawyers and the parties, to listen to it and make a determination about it. So I will say good evening to you and I will see you in the morning.

Testimony of Kenneth M. Monroe

Kenneth M. Monroe, first to testify, stated that he was off duty when he received the call at 10:33 p.m. on September 4, 1986. He got back into uniform and, as a Kansas highway patrol officer, began his investigation, one of two to three hundred he had investigated in his 17 years with the department.

On state and federal highways within his district, his jurisdiction was primary, though cooperation with local police and sheriff's officers was customary. The Kansas Highway Patrol is a separate department of state government, divided into districts, each served by at least one highly-qualified and well-trained patrolman whose primary duty is the "enforcement of traffic laws of this state relating to highways, vehicles, and drivers of vehicles."

The sheriff has similar duties within the several counties, as do the police departments of the cities within their city limits. Cooperation among the agencies is common, and the highway patrolman, because of qualifications, experience, and training, is given special deference where highways are involved.

Officer Monroe described the scene when he arrived as having 12 or so vehicles backed up, including the first of two ambulances. The highway was blacktop on a downhill grade at this point, with no shoulders. The federal government agencies dictate the current construction standard where financial participation is involved; however, many older highways, built before such standards, are permitted to remain in use. Such was the case of US Highway 77, connecting Marion and Florence. The cost of changing the grade or adding shoulders to this two-lane, blacktop highway would have exceeded its original cost and was simply not regarded as a priority in planning.

The officer's first task was to clear the area to prevent other accidents, then to examine the vehicles involved, take measurements and photographs, and, of course, to interview witnesses.

He did not complete his written report for several days. When asked of his contact with Ed Dilworth, he described for the jury the development of his determination of fault:

Mr. Dilworth kept interfering, he kept–he had told me his story of how the accident occurred, and the more I investigated the accident that evening, it didn't turn out to be or it wasn't turning out to be the way Mr. Dilworth said it was. And finally, I had to instruct Mr. Dilworth, especially when I was talking to Nathan, that I wanted Nathan to answer my question, not him. And he was persistent all through the investigation almost to the point of me having to tell him to keep away, he was interfering.

Officer Monroe continued that both of the Dilworths claimed that the impact was in the southbound lane, their lane, and that Sheryl was driving left of center and struck the trailer Nathan pulled behind the pickup. To the contrary, he determined that Nathan's pickup was left of center for a distance of 57.5 feet before the impact. There were no skid marks, gouges in the pavement, or scuff marks evident to verify in any way the story the Dilworths had agreed upon.

Nathan Dilworth in deposition testimony repeated that claim and, in fact, prepared a diagram indicating that Sheryl drove left of center, missed the pickup, but the left front of her car hit the left front corner of the trailer, becoming lodged there.

In keeping with his duty to inspect the scene, the officer stated that he carefully examined the road surface for any items having anything to do with the collision. He was asked and denied having seen (when daylight appeared or before) an audio cassette tape lying in plain sight within a foot of the roadway. This was significant in that Nathan and Ed took pictures of the scene showing a cassette tape along the highway in order to support their story.

Far from causing the collision, Sheryl was trying to escape from the pickup and trailer by going off the road entirely.

The homemade trailer, hauling an 11,000-pound backhoe, said Officer Monroe, had three axles, of which two, although equipped for brakes, had no brake shoes, which obviously rendered them of no use.

Another mechanical failure involved the ball hitch and mounting connecting the trailer and the pickup. The officer found the ball hitch bolt was still on the trailer and the nut was found by Ed Dilworth along the roadway and given to the officer. He examined the hole on the pickup rear mount and found the hole elongated around in a circle where the loose bolt had been working mainly backward and forward. The ball hitch itself was stripped of threads in different locations and other threads were damaged, which he stated would take a period of time to produce. He gave his opinion that a person driving a pickup towing a hitch in that condition would know that this motion was taking place, that the driver would feel this movement. He also stated that a driver feeling a trailer so loaded and swaying from side to side and whipping would realize that was happening. This swaying action was confirmed by a witness who met the rig and was fearful for her own safety. She testified later in the trial.

While the officer had no indication that any of the persons assisting him or aiding the victim at the scene were intoxicated, Ed Dilworth claimed that both investigators and emergency personnel had been drinking.

Cross-examination by Mr. Warta was routine until he made a mistake in asking the trooper about a driver's perception of a swaying trailer being towed. The trooper had just such an experience and testified that his notice of its occurrence came to him "just in a matter of seconds, sir," and that "my braking action was almost immediate." Of course, defense counsel quickly abandoned that line of pursuit, and, after a few perfunctory questions, ended his questioning.

Taking advantage of Mr. Warta's journey onto thin ice, Mr. Post asked the officer to repeat his experience with the loose trailer to emphasize that he applied his brakes immediately and stopped, even though the trailer struck his vehicle, and that he did not pass any other cars or continue driving down the road after it started weaving, thus laying the groundwork for the testimony of Theodora Koslowski to follow.

While Mr. Warta tried to negate speed on Nathan's part as negligence, he related it only to the prevailing speed limit of 55 mph. Mr. Post clarified that matter, as follows:

Q. *Several times Mr. Warta asked you about Nathan Dilworth and, according to what he said, that he wasn't exceeding the speed limit. And he asked you if speed played a part and you said that exceeding the speed limit did not play a part. How did speed play a part?*

A. *Under Kansas law, 8-1335, we have a law regarding driving at a speed greater than is reasonable and prudent. And it talks about hills; narrow, winding roadways, special conditions; hazardous conditions then existing at the time, including other traffic and pedestrians.*

Q. *And I believe you also testified you found no braking action by the pickup before the impact, no effective braking action from the vehicles?*

A. Yes sir, that is correct.

* * * [A question is repeated]

Q. *Yes, did you consider that the conditions on that night, with Nathan Dilworth driving the vehicle was, under the circumstances, required a reduced speed?*

A. *Yes, sir.*

Thereupon, Officer Monroe was released and Theodora Koslowski was called to the stand.

TESTIMONY OF THEODORA KOSLOWSKI

Theodora Koslowski immediately followed the testimony of Officer Monroe. A resident of Marion County all her 55 years, she was married to an employee of the Kansas Department of Transportation (responsible for highway maintenance), the mother of four children and was returning from a church meeting in Florence the night Sheryl died.

Mrs. Koslowski left for Marion about 10 to 20 minutes after 10 p.m. She preceded Sheryl down Highway 77 toward Marion. She described the highway, mentioned encountering another vehicle on the roadway, and described in her own words what she observed:

Well, I was coming over a hill and I was going down, then this other long hill was here and the vehicle came over the hill and it was going like this (indicating) and I thought, 'My word, what is happening?' and I slowed down and it kept coming and I pulled over as far as I could to the right side of the road, and then when it got to me it just slid back the other way or it would have been me.

When asked whether she had ever encountered anything like this vehicle, she said she had not. She arrived safely home and it was not until the following day that a member of the ambulance crew came in and commented that there had been "quite a wreck last night." She asked about it and he explained about the trailer. She then concluded, "I'm sure that I met that trailer when I came from Florence, pickup and trailer." She remembered there was something behind the pickup because it was swinging back and forth. Then Officer Monroe contacted her a few days later. Mrs. Koslowski did not know Sheryl and only later learned she had seen the Dilworths, who bought rock from the quarry where she worked, and she recalled them because they always paid cash, which was unusual. She also gave a statement to a State Farm adjuster and, by reference to it, corrected the time of her return to 15 to 20 minutes before 10 p.m. so that the collision with Sheryl happened just after Mrs. Koslowski passed the Dilworth pickup.

She concluded her responses to Mr. Post's questions about speed, saying:

Of course, I wouldn't have any way of knowing what speed they were going, but the way it was weaving, it seemed to me, "Oh, they should slow down before something happens." This is what she had also reported to the adjuster taking her statement. Cross-examination by Mr. Warta was merely conversation, producing nothing helpful to his position.

TESTIMONY OF GARY L. THOMPSON

Some explanation must introduce the next witness, an expert in accident reconstruction: Gary L. Thompson, of rural McPherson County. Even though State Farm insured both Sheryl and the Dilworths and therefore owed each a duty of fairness and equal treatment, its claims people had employed Mr. Thompson to investigate, without disclosing this to Sheryl's representatives and, practically speaking, concealed his report until discovery. When this came to our knowledge, we obtained a copy of his report. His testimony covered 54 pages of the trial record. His report and testimony raised serious questions about why State Farm continued to resist settlement.

Gary Thompson lived 7 miles north of McPherson, a town in central Kansas in what in local parlance would be called a mansion, fronted by a man-made pond of impressive size with acres of carefully landscaped and maintained grounds.

His employment was primarily as an engineering consultant in vehicular accident reconstruction. He holds a Ph.D. degree in aerospace engineering, with a minor in mathematics, and a specialty in structural dynamics. He was at this time in his 40s, a tall, handsome man. He had played basketball at the University of Kansas, a fact generally known throughout the state, which tended to add credibility to his responses.

Because he had been employed by Mr. Warta for the defense, we had a subpoena issued to compel his appearance at trial to dispel, as far as possible, any notion that we had in any way sanctioned State Farm's concealment.

Mr. Post began his questioning:

Q. *Now, you have received a subpoena to testify here in court today; is that correct?*

A. *That is correct.*

Q. *I believe that I called you and told you that a subpoena would be issued?*

A. *That's correct.*

Q. *And I also told you that because you were acting as a consultant for the investigators for Mr. Dilworth, that I would not discuss the case with you; is that correct?*

A. *That's also correct.*

Q. *So I have not had any discussions with you about the facts of the case or your findings in this case; is that correct?*

A. *That is true.*

Q. *And, likewise, the reporting that you did, you did not report any of your findings to either Eldon Bergeson or Marearl Denning, Sheryl Lynn Bergeson's parents; isn't that correct?*

A. *That's correct, I did not.*

Q. *And as a matter of fact, after you were retained to investigate the facts of this collision, you made reports that were directed only to Mr. Darrell Warta; isn't that correct?*

A. *That is correct.*

Q. *But you were contacted on September the 12th, the first contact, of 1986; is that correct? Or September the 11th?*

A. *That is correct.*

Q. *And that was by an investigator on behalf of Mr. Edward Dilworth; isn't that correct? Do you find a letter there of September 12?*

A. *That's correct.*

Q. *It was on behalf of Mr. Edward Dilworth, correct?*

A. *I assume that to be correct, I'm not sure of that.*

Q. *You were asked to make a detailed investigation to determine the point of impact of the two vehicles on the roadway; isn't that true?*

A. *Yes.*

(*Note by Don Shultz*: It is the sensitivity displayed to this point by the order of presentation of evidence and here, this hands-off and distant treatment of an insurance industry hireling, that distinguished Bradley Post as one of the truly great trial lawyers of this era.)

Under Kansas law, a witness qualifies to testify as an expert by reason of education or experience in an area beyond the common knowledge of humankind, and such experts are permitted to express matters of opinion based on such expertise, which is not allowed to other witnesses, whom we call "fact witnesses."

The fact of insurance is so far concealed from the jury that Mr. Post was allowed only to ask whether Mr. Thompson was employed "on behalf of Edward Dilworth," whether he furnished his report to Mr. Warta, and whether he reported any findings to either Eldon Bergeson or Marearl Denning. Mr. Thompson was employed to make a detailed investigation to determine the "point of impact," meaning the exact point at which some part of Sheryl's car and some point of the Dilworth trailer first came together.

In cross-examination, the attorney is permitted to ask questions that are leading and suggestive, in which the answer is suggested, and the witness is led to answer in the form and order controlled by his examiner. Leading questions otherwise are subject to objection as we have previously noted.

Gary Thompson testified by way of opinion from his records, which included references to the ball hitch bolt and nut, and a diagram, marked Plaintiff's Exhibit 4, which he had prepared, identifying the several points of significance, (which is copied in the appendix.) He testified that the 1978 Ford pickup was pulling a 25-foot trailer loaded with a backhoe. The pickup put down 157 feet of skidmarks, starting in the southbound lane, in which 45 feet led to the center line of the highway, indicating 90 feet approximately left of center, that is, in Sheryl's lane of travel. The point of impact between the trailer and Sheryl's little car was 8 feet from the center line in her lane. The loaded trailer intruded approximately 12 inches into Sheryl's car.

The hole in which the ball hitch had been inserted was

elongated from frequent motion. The threads on the bolt were stripped in places, and sheared and mashed in others. The nut could be slipped on the shank with no screw action. Mr. Thompson stated significantly that, "if there is a loose ball hitch, you would know it."

Of course, basic to claims for punitive damages is the existence of knowledge of the danger and continuing with such knowledge in callous disregard of the consequences, especially to innocent victims.

Gary Thompson had inquired about the existence of a lock washer on the hitch. Nathan insisted there had been. Both Trooper Monroe and the sheriff reported that no lock washer was found.

In response to a question based on the account of the collision as reported by Nathan, Mr. Thompson first revealed that he had relied on the point of impact established by Officer Monroe, because the indicating marks from the highway surface were no longer identifiable by the time he was asked to reconstruct the accident. When tested on the physical probability of Nathan's account showing Sheryl crossing the center line, striking the corner of the trailer, which was then driven backward by force 90 feet and, once loosed, traveled in the opposite direction back up the hill, where it was found turned around heading south, he called such an account "highly unlikely." He agreed that yaw marks and side-scuffing marks would be evident in such a case and that none were found.

His charges were about $2,400.

In cross-examination, Mr. Warta proved more productive trying to get his money's worth. Thompson's account of the instructions given by the insurer sounded noble enough: "to determine the speed of the vehicles, if possible, as well as whether or not any of the drivers took evasive action." After lamenting the fact that he had not seen the ball hitch before preparing his report, he estimated the pickup's speed at no more than 51 mph, keeping it under the 55 mph limit in existence at that time. He gave no speed for Sheryl's vehicle. Mr. Thompson then returned to the theme of being kept from seeing the ball hitch. He surmised that a lock washer had come free, allowing movement to begin in the hitch assembly. The fact that no washer was found did not seem to impair his scientific reasoning. His explanation went like this: The lock washer failed and "the trailer would start oscillating very slightly, . . . you would not sense it in the vehicle until the trailer out-tracked sufficiently to get a side-loading on the tires to get a scuffing. It would increase the load and pull it one way or the other. When it gets to that point, it's just about, frankly, all over and this happens in a matter of seconds. It's not a thing that happens over a long period of time. The small oscillations can go on for a while, but the big oscillations, that person would sense that in the vehicle and you just will not sense them very long. It's a matter of seconds and you will have separation and failure."

Of course, this scenario, if believed, would relieve the Dilworths of much of the charge of callous indifference and disregard of the dangers. However, coming as it did after Officer Monroe's experience with a boat trailer and Theodora Koslowski's encounter with the weaving trailer at least more than "seconds" from the contact with Sheryl had the effect rather of casting Gary Thompson as a hireling and his testimony as partisan.

On re-direct examination, Bradley put the stinger on him by having him testify to this question:

Q. *And at no time in either of your reports you got this $2400 from the representatives of the Dilworths– in your reports did you say anything about any possible failure of a lock washer, did you, sir?*

A. *I mentioned in paragraph A of my second report what was available to look ...*

Q. *And what you said is, "There is no accompanying lock washer," correct?*

A. *That's precisely correct.*
Q. *And you did not say anything, when you wrote this second report after you inspected this carefully, you didn't say anything about seeing evidence that a lock washer had ever been present, did you, sir?*
A. *That's correct.*

Mr. Thompson had only heard from Nathan Dilworth about a lock washer during a recess in the trial, and although he was questioned further by Mr. Warta, the rest of his testimony did not change the facts.

The trial was recessed by Judge Theis for the day. What the jury made of Mr. Thompson and his testimony is an open question for the jurors.

TESTIMONY OF DONNA SILL

Donna Sill, Sheryl's supervising teacher in her practicum, next appeared and testified.

I live in Manhattan, Kansas, and teach fourth grade at Riley County Grade School northwest of Manhattan. I have taught for three years.

In order to receive certification as an elementary teacher, 125 to 140 hours of classes, of which at least 40 are in education courses, is required. One semester of practice teaching is required.

Practice teaching at K-State means you are in a classroom setting in which you teach for half a day every day for eight weeks. Then, for the other eight weeks, you are in school for the entire day, and during that time you add more classes that you teach, until the last four weeks you are teaching the entire course the whole day while the supervising teacher is observing.

I have been a 'cooperating' teacher two times, meaning a teacher in charge of a student taking practice teaching.

Sheryl Lynn Bergeson became my student teacher in January of 1986. She came to school a few days ahead to meet me before she was to start.

It was my first experience as cooperating teacher. Sheryl was with me from January until May, 1986.

After Sheryl's funeral, I wrote the following letter to her mother."

Q. *Do you think you might be able to read it for the jury?*

A. *Might take a while. I can try.*

She reads, pausing occasionally to regain control of her emotions, verging on tears:

Dear Mr. and Mrs. Denning,

I am writing this letter in hopes that maybe it will help you to know, more than you do already, how special Sheryl was. I do not mean to upset you further and I pray that I don't. I met Sheryl this past January when she walked into my class to do her student teaching. I liked her immediately. She was here only a matter of weeks and I had come to consider her my friend. By the time she left in May, I loved her as a sister. She had the same affect on my kids. They all loved her.

She was a wonderful teacher. She had a sense of humor, a touch of the dramatic, a knowledge of life, and a smile that made the kids do anything she asked. She was the "Pied Piper" of Riley. I feel sorry for the kids who did not have the chance to have her for their teacher. She was truly blessed.

As for myself, I came to know Sheryl quite well during the semester. She was cheerful, vibrant, goofy, serious, fun, loving, whimsical, mature, crazy, and caring, all rolled into one. We poured our souls out to one another and never worried about anyone else finding out what we said. We had a mutual trust. She took care of my daughter like she'd been doing it for years. She loved family, and when she spoke of her own, her eyes lit up. She loved you all very much. I know I do not feel half the sorrow that you do. I do thank God for letting me know Sheryl and have a part of her even if only for a short nine months. I know as you do that she is with God now. She hurts for us, and I know if she could, she'd hug us and tell us to be happy because she hated it when we were sad. We will see Sheryl again in our thoughts and memories, our hearts, and when we go to God, also.

Donna continued her testimony saying,

In trying to let her find out my way of teaching and trying to find out her way of teaching and seeing, because teachers can learn from their student teachers, as well as students learning from their cooperating teachers, we both learned a lot from each other.

We became really good friends. I had a brand-new baby and she just absolutely adored her. She came over and babysat for me, and we spent a lot of time together. She asked me would I please leave so she could have the baby. She said she always liked kids and she always wanted to be around kids. And when she first started college, she wanted to be a commercial artist, but her professors said she lacked that level required, so she decided on teaching. Then she said she couldn't see herself doing anything besides teaching.

She had to turn in her lesson plans every Friday for the next week. I would look them over and discuss them. There were few times she had to ask for anything. If it came up she needed to change, she was always flexible. And when she took over the actual teaching, I was almost jealous of her because they became 'her kids' instead of mine. The kids loved her. We have one little girl who was especially attached to Sheryl. She still talks about her to her sister.

I gauged her potential as an elementary teacher better than mine. At that time I thought she was going to be great, a master teacher.

She was interested in sports and went to the track coach and asked to help. There was a group of 8th graders called "Miss Bergeson's Fan Club," and I'm sure there were 50 to 75 kids at her funeral because that's how many kids she affected at our school.

She was good at discipline. She had a plan, what steps you take, and what punishment if you break the rules, and she let the kids make the rules.

Her attendance was excellent. She had certain days for classes, and she was allowed to go to interviews for her employment, and one day her grandfather passed away, and then the day she died. Otherwise, she was always there.

My husband worked in the oil fields, and when he was on a rig he was gone for two weeks or a month at a time, and Sheryl would come over. She came over a lot and it was just us three girls, Sheryl and me and the baby. And when my husband got some time off, he was there, too, and he got really attached to her.

The end of May or the first of June she came over to tell me that she was leaving for the summer. She had got the job she had applied for and she wrote me a letter to tell me. She said she would give me a call, "You'll need to help me out because I am going to need your help."

I learned about her death from our school secretary. She called me into the office, took me into the nurse's office, and closed the door. So I knew the news was bad. She said, "I have some bad news for you." I said, "Just tell me and get it over with." She said, "Sheryl is dead." And I have two friends, I had Sheryl and another friend named Sheryl, and I said, "Which Sheryl?" And she said, "Sheryl Bergeson." And I said, "No, she's not." And she said she was in a car accident that night, and they didn't know any of the details but she was dead.

Of course, I had to announce to her students about her death. I found a few of them and got them in a circle, and when I told them they acted a lot like I am right now (weeping).

I had met her mom briefly at the graduation and we went over to her apartment afterwards. She loved peach-colored roses, so I gave her some to tell her "hi" and "congratulations."

TESTIMONY OF MICHAEL BALDWIN

Michael Baldwin, called next, was a classroom teacher for eight years before qualifying as an administrator. He testified that he met Sheryl first while at Great Bend in a junior high school. She was a freshman. She applied for and was given the job of team manager for the girls' basketball team, which he coached. He learned from her teachers a lot of good things about her. He had during his coaching a lot of team managers and one that was extraordinary. The manager must come early and stay late after practice; get things set up for practice, stay late to put things away. She was, without a doubt, the best manager he ever had. She was dedicated to the sport and the team, and was a dependable asset to the program. She was well-organized and took athletics seriously as a part of the education. While she was manager and he was coach, the girls' team had a record of 106 wins and 13 losses. He felt the team manager was every bit as important as the best player. She had the ability to lay out a timely schedule and to do the things which needed to be done. With her organization and skill in getting things ready, all that he had to do was to be there to coach.

Mike Baldwin knew also that Sheryl was an outstanding student who made the honor rolls, and her academic and social skills were impeccable. She was the type of student every teacher enjoyed and the type of young lady every father would wish his daughter to be. She was a leader in her classes, served on the yearbook staff and student council, and captained her track team (a position voted by the players). She was extremely active and succeeded at all she put her hand to.

In 1986 Mike Baldwin was principal of the schools in Marion when Sheryl applied for a teaching position. Vacancies were circulated to placement offices in universities in and out of the state. When he and other administrators were at K-State looking for teachers for USD 408, Marion-Florence, Sheryl dropped by to see if positions were open. A 7th and 8th grade math position was open and she applied.

The hiring in most cases was left to the principals, but the superintendent, John Burke, asked that when a top-notch candidate applied, that he be contacted so he could personally arrange an interview. When Sheryl applied, this procedure was followed. Sheryl was their top choice. She was offered the contract and she accepted.

They had interviewed others but were pleased when Sheryl accepted. Mr. Baldwin observed that her personality had not changed since junior high school. She was responsible, outgoing, motivated; she had leadership qualities and was highly organized. The high expectations she set for herself were simply not found in first-year teachers. He found her enthusiastic about teaching. She wanted to work with students and the one concern about the position at Florence was whether there would be any coaching available at the time.

Mrs. Reed, the volleyball coach, was very impressed with her ability to work with the students, and Sheryl was able to get along well with the staff members. Her rapport with both students and teachers was very positive, and the entire staff felt a loss at her death.

On September 4, 1986, there was an open house scheduled at the Florence middle school to get students and their parents to visit the classroom teachers and observe some activities planned for the school year, so that parents would feel comfortable about contacting the school concerning any problems that might arise. Mike Baldwin attended that open house and had an easy opportunity to observe her during the course of the evening, her room being directly across from his office. She got along very well. There were no problems.

He left Florence headed for Marion ahead of Sheryl and only learned of the tragedy by a call from one of the nurses at the hospital seeking an identification. Before he could arrive, they had found Sheryl's billfold and made a satisfactory identification. He was asked to provide information about her parents. From his acquaintance with them at Great Bend, he found information about her father. He called Eldon and simply told him to call the hospital. Local ministers were contacted to be at the school the next morning to manage the crisis for the school day.

The school staff that was free, including Mr. Baldwin (principal), Mr. Burke (superintendent), Mrs. Reed (the volleyball coach), and a special education teacher attended the funeral. A special service was later held at the school for students unable to attend. A memorial was established in her honor, and Eldon, her father, was able to attend to present the award. While her mother was not able to be present because of employment obligations, Mr. Baldwin wrote her a letter enclosing a copy of the newspaper article and accompanying picture of the event. Both the article and a copy of his letter were made exhibits in the case. Exhibits of this kind, called "real evidence," are marked numerically or alphabetically and are added to the transcript of oral testimony to complete the record in the case. The jury is allowed to take exhibits which are admitted to the jury room for their deliberations.

There was no cross-examination of Mr. Baldwin, there being little hope of doing any more than to enforce the gracious esteem in which he held Sheryl.

TESTIMONY OF ROBERT D. LINDER

History professor Robert D. Linder, from Kansas State University, having taught a combined total of 30 years, told of his regard for Sheryl, who had taken three of his courses. She made A's in two and a B in the third. In connection with one of these courses, History of Christianity, he had a standing policy of inviting any students who wished to lunch with him on a certain day. Sometimes this involved groups, but at other times just Sheryl and some of her friends. On several occasions, she related that she had been studying the Bible on her own and, as a result, he had become a little closer to her than to some of the other students. "She was an exceptional young woman, in love with life, and she had an infectious smile. And just the kind of student I decided to come back to Kansas State so I could teach."

He thought her "just cut out for elementary teaching, just made for the profession." He wrote a reference for Sheryl as a part of her credentials for placement. He also wrote her parents after learning of her death and enclosed a copy of her essay written for his Christianity course. He read these to the jury.

Testimony of John Burke

John Burke, mentioned previously by Michael Baldwin, was in his fifth year as superintendent of schools for Marion County during Sheryl's tenure at the Florence Middle School. He held bachelor's and master's degrees in physical education and was in the process of completing his doctorate in curriculum instruction from Kansas State University. He had considerable previous experience having taught in both Arizona and Colorado. It was part of his duties to interview and recommend teachers for positions in Marion County.

Mr. Burke became acquainted with Sheryl in the spring of 1986 when filling the vacancy for a math teacher at Florence Middle School. He identified the needs a prospective teacher must submit. These were marked and offered into evidence. He described the interview and his impression of Sheryl: "She was vivacious. She had a vitality about her that would light up a room. She was very pleasant, bright, and very polite."

In filling positions, it was not uncommon to have a hundred applicants. In order to narrow the prospects, the first step was to review the credentials, which could include her teaching certificate from the state, her academic transcript, medical records, and the like. By reviewing this information, the number of applicants to actually be interviewed was narrowed down to five candidates. Of Sheryl's credentials, he responded, "Her credentials were top-notch."

When they offered Sheryl the contract and she accepted, his response was, "I was thrilled. Any time we can get a teacher of her caliber with her potential for growth, we are ecstatic."

Sheryl had written with her application:

I feel that my credentials could greatly benefit your school district in many ways. First, my student teaching practice was located at Riley, Kansas, a small district north of Manhattan. I enjoyed teaching in a smaller setting. I felt I could get to know the students better.

Math is a very important subject and I feel I can relate these concepts to children at a concrete level.

I enjoy teaching. I am looking for a challenge and something I can call my own. Education is very valuable and should be handled with great care. I intend on doing just that.

He repeated the history Mike Baldwin had given him of his contact with Sheryl in the school system at Great Bend, where she was basketball manager for Mr. Baldwin during her freshman year. This held an obvious appeal for Mr. Burke, given his degrees in physical education. Her interest in athletics and her listing as assistant instructor in volleyball also commended her in his eyes.

Mr. Burke met Sheryl occasionally in Manhattan and in those visits she expressed her devotion to her sisters and her parents. He saw her as being a potential master teacher, a mentor to other new teachers, a standing he reserved only to the top 10 percent of all applicants.

He had the practice of dropping in unannounced to observe classrooms in session. When he entered Sheryl's classroom, he observed that the eyes of every student were on her. He watched for two minutes and there were no disruptions, no distractions, no activity but the students watching her. In volleyball, the B-team players idolized her. They thought she was just fantastic.

John Burke was shocked to learn of Sheryl's death. He arranged for local ministers to be paired up with each teacher when her death was reported to the students to help them process their feelings about her death. He discouraged students from attending her funeral services because of the distance from Florence but, to provide closure for them, he arranged with ministers to come back to the school and hold a memorial service for the students to attend.

The students basically idolized her. It's infrequent that you find teachers that the students will relate to instantly and Sheryl was one of these.

After the direct examination, the court asked, "I assume you have no cross, Mr. Warta?" His response, "No, Your Honor."

Testimony of Marearl Denning

The next witness was Sheryl's mother, Marearl Denning. The questions were couched to call forth small, concise responses. Often overlapping, they were designed to allow a loving mother to expand on her loss of an exceptional daughter.

Sheryl had a special place in her heart for her step-sister, Bianca, and her half-sister, daughter of Eldon and Donna, Candice. Sheryl spent a lot of time teaching her. She was always interested in taking care of her younger sisters and was counted on to be very reliable in that regard.

The family tradition was that the oldest grandchild passed out the gifts at Christmas. Sheryl's strong personality and natural leadership made her good at that job. As she got older, she graduated to helping her mother plan family dinners, for which she would often place hearts on the table. It was a comfort to both sides of the divided family to have Sheryl there, helpful and dependable, providing advice and counsel to her sisters. The advice was of a kind which might have been rejected if coming from a parent but was taken from Sheryl, whom they saw as their role model and leader. Her pride in her sisters was reflected in their pride in her. If they had questions about school or anything else, she was always objective and supportive and always worked with them toward a solution to help them see another side of things. Sheryl regularly expressed interest in her sisters' education and indicated a willingness to help financially when they attended college.

As with her mother and her sisters, Sheryl also loved her father, Eldon, very much. She was proud of him and gave him her respect and admiration. Of course, he was a wonderful father, as well–compassionate, nurturing, and intelligent. Marearl kept a baby book for Sheryl, which was passed to the jury, titled, "All About Me." Recorded were her heights and weights, when she received her shots, her first prayer, the history of teaching her to say grace before meals, pictures with various family members at birthdays, her favorite stories and toys. Her first word was "daddy."

What emerged from the testimony of her family and those who knew her best was summed up by the jury foreman's reply when asked whether they wished to take her picture to the jury room, "We don't need it. We know she was an angel!"

Testimony of William T. Terrell

William T. Terrell, an expert economist, testified for the purpose of establishing in the minds of the jury the financial benefit over an expected lifetime from a person like Sheryl, but for her untimely death.

After a lengthy qualification process to establish his standing to give credible evidence on this point, Dr. Terrell began to project the amounts Sheryl would earn in her career employment as a teacher. Bradley had prepared an exhibit he intended to offer reflecting the present value of those future earnings and the amount Sheryl would be expected to use for her own needs, leaving an amount that would be available to her to assist her parents, which would be direct benefits to them, or to her sisters, which would relieve the parents of these obligations, called indirect benefits.

Bradley asked Dr. Terrell to refer to the blowup of Exhibit 32, which he intended to offer to form the basis for economic damages recoverable as an element of damages enumerated in the instructions the court would give the jury. Upon making reference to the exhibit, Mr. Warta objected and requested a side-bar conference outside the hearing of the jury. The argument extended and the court dismissed the jury for the rest of that afternoon.

The basic objection was that there was no expectation on the part of Eldon and Marearl that Sheryl would make contributions in the future, that it was speculative whether she would do so, and that the introduction of figures to the jury of a million dollar income plus $230,000 in fringe benefits would be prejudicial.

Bradley, of course, argued to the court that he had no intention of urging the jury to adopt these total figures as damages but simply to use them to form a basis for allowance of such damages should the jury believe from all the testimony that Sheryl was likely to make valuable contributions. After lengthy argument, the court considered what is called an "offer of proof," which can be done in one of several ways. One, counsel may recite what the witness would testify to if called; 2) the witness may be presented live before the court in the absence of the jury; 3) if he had testified in a discovery deposition, the court could simply read the deposition. But none had been taken, so Bradley presented Dr. Terrell live.

The argument to the court, abbreviated somewhat, went as follows:

Mr. Warta: *The cases in Kansas are clear that if you are going to allow any pecuniary damage that ties up with somebody's loss of earnings, there has got to be substantial evidence of a reasonable basis for expectation of future monetary benefits. What I'm saying is that there is no expectation that they were going to get any loss of earnings, a possibility, we don't have any idea . . . .*

The Court: [finishing his sentence] . . . *how much."*

Mr. Warta: *This is absolutely, purely speculative to put in an exhibit that shows she would have made a million dollars and another $230,000. It's purely prejudicial.*

Mr. Post: *The Marcourt case was the basis for the Wentling, as to what would have been available.*

The Court: *Well, you are both partly right and partly wrong. It does take after Marcourt, and that's a later case, you're referring to the Wentling case?*

Mr. Post: *Yeah.*

The Court: *But if we're dealing with children, minor children, you don't have much of a problem, for a while, at least.* (Meaning that the death of a parent while that person's children are minors, a reasonable expectation follows that a major portion of the parent's income would have been used for their care and support, arising, if from nothing else, the obligation that the law imposes on parents to provide such support.) *But if the question is, what happens when you have an adult child? And that's where the difference is. I don't know that there is too much damage as he suggests in putting the evidence in. I may have to knock it out and tell them [the jury] to disregard the amounts. The fact she makes a million dollars a year, she's certainly not going to give them a million dollars.*

Mr. Post: *And I will point out, then, above her living expenses, what she would have available, if she chose.*

The Court: *Then you have to translate, don't you, to some amount she would have given?*

Mr. Post: *I don't think so . . . it would be totally voluntary.*

The Court: *Let's have a recess here.* (The court, at this point, excuses the jury to go to the jury room, explaining:) *We have a matter we should have processed before now. It affects the admission of evidence here, so, if you will retire to the jury room. We'll call you back.*

The Court (continuing after jury is gone:) *Well, let's carry on here. Let's assume, Mr. Post, I let this evidence in about it, which shows she makes a lot of money. How do you tie it up with what amount the parents might get in the future? That's the weak link in your chain, as I see it.*

Mr. Post: *I'm not going to ask him to testify as to specific amounts, no.*

The Court: *How are you going to relate to the specific well, you have to show a financial loss. We are not dealing with minor children, we are dealing with an adult daughter and adult parents. I'm not fond of this particular law, but I don't make the law. I am bound by what the law is, as you know.*

Mr. Post: *Well, Judge, it is a fact that when you begin, all of the economic benefits flow from the parent to the child, but as the child reaches maturity, at a point, it starts going the other way.*

The Court: *Okay.*

Mr. Post: *And, depending on that child, sometimes the need is great, sometimes it's not great.*

The Court: *Well, you just put your finger on the speculative nature, haven't you?*

The discussion continued in this same vein for sometime, with Bradley arguing that the Wentling case, which he had tried to a jury and which had successfully stood appeal from a very substantial verdict applied.

The plaintiff, of course, has the duty to show his case is more probably true than not true, and that standard applies to damages as well as other factual issues. In this case, although the judge did not express it in these terms, there was no evidence that the parents would need or that it was probable that either of them would become needy in the foreseeable future, whether Sheryl would have responded to that need or not. Failing such evidence, offering figures of her future earnings would invite speculation on the part of the jury and could result in serious trial error, reversing any verdict, and necessitating retrial of the case, the judge saying,

I think your evidence under these circumstances is prejudicial if I let it go to the jury.

Thereafter, the jury was excused for the rest of the day, and Professor Terrell was returned to the stand to offer evidence outside the hearing of the jury in what is called an "offer of proof." The court then considers the evidence and, if it concludes it is admissible, it is then presented live to the jury. If not, then the objection made to it is sustained and it is kept from the jury.

Dr. Terrell's testimony for this purpose included a projection of future earnings for Sheryl, referring to life expectancy tables for her life and the lives of her parents. Sheryl at age 22 had a life expectancy of "50-some" years with a work life of 45 years. He calculated the life expectancy from Sheryl's death for Marearl at 39 years and for Eldon, at 41-42 years.

The professor had prepared a chart reflecting the figure he was being called to testify about, identified as Exhibit 32, entitled, "Estimated Lifetime Labor Compensation for Sheryl Lynn Bergeson," dated July 31, 1989. (This date was the prior trial date, which had changed, the exhibit being computed to an exact date.) The calculations included what Sheryl would have earned over the life expectancy of her mother and father, based on her base salary as a teacher. There was no enhancement or increase for other, more highly-paid, employment. He also expressed the opinion that had Sheryl wished, she would have had summer employment and better employment than teaching. Any funds not needed for her living expenses would have been available for use on behalf of other persons. While the actual use for others would depend on her willingness, Dr. Terrell declined to offer an opinion on this,

"I'm not an expert on willingness."

He testified that a number of things an adult child would do for her parents would have economic value, including time spent in doing anything on their behalf, as well as time spent in phone calls, traveling to visit them, and executing other transactions in their interest. He characterized such services as like "the fire department, you don't need them until you need them and you know they're there." But the real activity comes in later years when people get beyond their age of working and certain debilitations set in. That's when the attention and service and time from a child becomes very important. He did not attempt to put a dollar amount on the value of these services, but he nevertheless affirmed that they have economic value. While some little services can be purchased in the marketplace and valued in this way, the unique confidence and trust of parent and child cannot be purchased.

The proffer continued at some length and the court announced that he would rule on the objection on the following morning, which he did.

The Court: *I don't have any objection to your economist testifying that these have economic value, but I'm not going to let you use that damn chart. It will be error, and you can't convert non-pecuniary damages into pecuniary damages, and that's what you want to do.*

So that's what happened. Professor Terrell was recalled and the jury heard his testimony, much as in the offer of proof as to those things that had economic value.

The court's ruling was governed by Federal Rule of Evidence 1006, which was entirely at the discretion of the court and which would not be disturbed on an appeal except for an abuse of that discretion. Thus ended this lengthy scene backstage.

It should be noted that this argument consumed 92 pages of the court transcript in this case. Mr. Ames, the Dilworths' attorney, took no part in this argument and was heard very little during the trial. In these proceedings, counsel speaking usually stand while the other party remains seated. When proceedings take place in the judge's chambers (his office), however, proceedings tend to be less formal and the attorneys remain seated. The clients may or may not be present during these sessions, depending on the attorneys' wishes.

Charts, graphs, and exhibits that provide visuals for testimony that is otherwise admissible are ordinarily admitted without controversy. However, if their content is remote or speculative, or tends to mislead the jury, the judge may at his discretion refuse their admission.

Bradley's theory that juries decide how much they want to allow and simply find places to put it in the verdict form is pretty much borne out by the fact that the jury allowed $50,000 for economic loss to her parents.

When the trial resumed, Dr. Terrell testified to various elements of a loving daughter's service to her parents which had economic value, which were covered in the discussion of the "in camera" argument. Mr. Warta's cross-examination addressed the fact that a 22-year-old daughter would from her earnings provide a home, food, and clothing; pay taxes, transportation, and utilities, and so forth. Then Mr. Warta covered the same list as to marriage and later children to dissipate the quantity of funds available for other purposes. When he came to the availability of time, that is, the free time or spare time a child would have available to parents, the following exchange led to a question by the judge:

Q. *And another thing you're talking about is time. And again, to the extent that someone is employed, that takes away time that they could otherwise be using for their parents. Would you agree with that?*

A. *Well, that's just one aspect of it.*

Q. *Just one aspect?*

A. *Ordinarily, we think of giving up time from all our pursuits. Going on a trip for vacation or whatever, in the interest of employment.*

The Court [to the witness]*: Just saying that if you are employed, you are employed and have a job and teaching school, whatever, that is time that you are committed to that you can't use to take care of parents?*

A. *Yes, sir. The teaching time commitment, though, we understand to be only nine months of the year.*

It is always of special interest when the judge questions a witness. When he does it in the flow of testimony adduced by one of the attorneys, as here, apparently to clarify the meaning of an answer, he acts almost as a voice for the jury, since it cannot question witnesses during the trial. The usual judicial attitude is that the lawyers should try the case. So when this happens, attention is drawn to the exchange. The judge is not trying to influence the case in any way, but it is important that he, himself, understand.

The witness also took good care for his position as a witness for the party who hired him. In responding to the question of whether there would be little need from a daughter where the parents were able to take care of themselves economically, he responded:

It would lessen the money flow. It would not lessen the flow of availability, being on-call like a fire department, being ready in case something happened.

The simile of the fire department was especially effective in demonstrating and persuading the jury that the services themselves have economic value, but equally important is the value of availability.

Despite the court's rejection of Exhibit 32, on re-direct examination, Bradley was able to get in the amount of Sheryl's nine-months' earnings, her special skills, and her history of regular employment, that she would doubtless find employment in the off-months, and that, while her wages as a teacher would gradually increase, the witness thought it likely that she would change to other employment which would ordinarily result in a "big jump."

Mr. Warta then attempted to take the sting from this testimony by suggesting Sheryl's love for teaching would have kept her in that profession, regardless of the lure to higher pay.

Dr. Terrell was then excused and Sheryl's father, Eldon Bergeson, was called.

Testimony of Eldon Bergeson

The contrast of the testimony of her father, Eldon Bergeson, with the testimony of her mother earlier, serves to illustrate the truth that their genetic contribution to the birth is nothing as compared to the personality likeness of each developed in Sheryl's childhood. All of the sweet intimacy and delight of the mother-daughter are contrasted with the father's contribution of athletic skill and competitive ambition instilled in this remarkable young woman.

Eldon and Marearl were classmates when the high schools in their rural communities were consolidated. Her name was Bahr and, in those days, as he said, "There wasn't much imagination, so all the B's sat together," putting him close to Marearl. They married after high school, and Sheryl was born on July 27, 1964, "almost on the way to Emporia, Kansas, to the hospital."

By March or April 1969, they had lived in several places in Nebraska and moved to Great Bend, Kansas, where Sheryl began her early schooling. He remembered with regret that his employment and the growing family of girls caused him to divide what little time he had for his family among them. He recognized her early artistic gifts, and noted her activities in piano and swimming lessons and the variety of activities common to children.

His testimony was aided with visuals: scrapbooks, pictures, artistic creations, and the like, which were living illustrations of the things Sheryl herself prized, things found among her belongings after her death. Eldon was permitted to stand before the jury and, turning page by page, comment on the progress and development of Sheryl's life. In it, the father's pride, gentleness, and love came flowing so that he did not have to describe the pain at learning of her death, at not having some little time with her before being able to pour out to her his pride and love.

Her scrapbook included newspaper clippings about basketball and football, not always things that she participated in but things that interested her. She recorded her pen pal correspondence with a girl from Germany and a contest she won in grade school drawing ads for local businesses. Sheryl recorded the letter she was awarded in track in the 7th grade, inserted with a picture of her sister Donelle and a picture of the 7th grade track team. Also included was a picture of two of Mr. Baldwin's basketball teams that he had testified about. A vast variety of the items related to track, baseball, and scholastics, such as a student council election she took part in. He was especially moved by the Junior Olympics, for which he provided the transportation, saying "This was a time that just the two of us spent together."

Among her achievements, besides the variety of athletics, was high school journalism, as ad manager for the school paper and yearbook. She did drawing and weaving. He identified a weaving done on plexiglass. She would lay out the design and "Dad would cut it out and drill about 3,000 holes in it so she could weave through the plexiglass."

Sheryl's spiritual experiences included regularly attending Sunday school and church services, as well as vacation Bible school, where she later helped in some teaching, and MYF (Methodist Youth Fellowship). She was later active in the Fellowship of Christian Athletes (FCA), serving as treasurer when Marearl was a Sunday school teacher for Sheryl's class. He said:

Sheryl often helped me prepare for these classes (4th and 5th grades). Sometimes she would ask what we were going to study, and then she would help other students find the verses, etc.

She wasn't looking for "stars in her crown," just being helpful.

Scholastic achievements and other school-related activities

included an offer of a partial scholarship to play ball at the University of Kansas. She won first place for an ad layout in regional competition sponsored by the Kansas Scholastic Press Association; the previous year she had won third place, as a junior. She was a candidate for homecoming queen. In this competition, she listed these activities: Panther Tales staff ad manager, track, pep club and pep club president, Kayettes, student council, scholastic art award, homecoming attendant, FCA and FCA treasurer.

Again in the area of sports, she participated in shot-put and discus, Eldon said, adding: *And sometimes they have a competition with all the weight men, really which means all the people that are normally in weight events; it's limited to those people that participate in weight events, and she ran in those relays occasionally.*

While her mother had said Sheryl beat her father's record in the shot-put and discus, Eldon corrected that error, as follows:

I would like to take this opportunity to correct that error. I think she lacked about 12 or 14 feet of bettering my record. The real competition was between her younger sister Kristin who was always trying to better Sheryl's records.

Seeing her father's size, about half again hers, as shown by his daughter's pictures, it would be difficult indeed to visualize Sheryl out-distancing him in the weight competitions.

The softball teams she played on, both in Great Bend and later in Wyoming, were not the slow-pitch variety so popular nowadays, but fast-pitch, which is a more challenging skill. She started in the outfield, but later became the regular catcher. In a letter to her sister Donelle, she comments on the problem of adjusting on the women's team in Wyoming to the use of the smaller ball than that she was accustomed to hitting. She also reported in that letter that her team won third place in the tournament at

Evanston (Wyoming), adding: *We should've been second, but we just couldn't hit the ball.*

Regarding her eagerness to be employed, her father recited her employment in Wyoming for the pipeline company and various other jobs, such as with Big Cheese Pizza and Godfather's Pizza, both in Great Bend. At one time, she asked her father to teach her how to mow the lawn so that she could hire out to the neighbors. He related that experience:

And so the first time I said, 'Okay, Sheryl, you mow our lawn and I will pay you and you can go into business! And the first time she mowed it, she hit the manhole cover on the water meter and bent the crankshaft on the mower and cost me a new motor on the mower. But after a dismal start, she did mow lawns.

To list all the honors, awards, and recognition Sheryl received in her outstanding young life would protract to boredom. It is sufficient that the portrayal of her life accurately and adequately described an amazing young woman. It would be to stop unfairly short in her father's testimony, however, to omit two incidents: one in childhood concerning a neighbor and the second as a young adult concerning her grandfather.

When Sheryl and Kristin were little they would wander around the block to the house of a little lady named Mabel Strobel. She went to the same church, and when they would visit she seemed to have milk and cookies to serve them and flowers for them to take home. When Mrs. Strobel saw that Sheryl was to graduate from high school, she sent this touching little note:

Hello, Sheryl. Our paths never cross, but you have no idea how often I think of you. I am proud of you, your name is always on the honor roll, you are so talented in art, too. Here you are a senior with big plans for next year and the future. Keep up the good work.

I love you. Mabel Strobel

The second narrative involved her grandfather, Louis Bergeson, who continued to live in Leonardville after selling his farm. Found among his possessions after his death was this note from Sheryl:

Dear Grandpa,

Hello, how are you? I am fine. I'm still keeping busy in school. Before long, classes will be through and I will be out for Christmas break. I got your letter. I'm sorry it has taken so long to return one. I understand your reasons for staying in Great Bend. I just want you to know the door is open here and I will do anything to help you with your living arrangements. I don't want you to feel as if I am trying to pressure you, I just want you to be happy, yet safe. And I don't think you are an old crab. How have you been feeling? I hope this letter finds you in good condition. Have you heard from Shirley or Shelly or Mike? Well, I was curious to know if any of them offered to come and get you for Thanksgiving or just mentioned it. Well, I am coming to Great Bend over Thanksgiving and I will get there Thursday night or Tuesday night before Thanksgiving and will be there until Sunday. Maybe I could take you to Mike's for Thanksgiving dinner or something. Just let me know what you hear and we can make some plans. I talked to Donna this weekend and I guess she got my airline ticket for Christmas break. Have you thought any more about going with me? I would really like you to go and the rest of the family would be thrilled. Well I better get back to my studies.

Take care, I love you lots,
Sheryl

What might the parents of such a child have expected to benefit from her future care if she was willing to "open her door" to her 78-year-old Grandpa?

Though we might well add the help she was to her father following the divorce when she helped care for her younger sisters, we will only add that when asked whether they admired Sheryl, Kristin said,

Are you kidding? We worshiped her. Everything Sheryl wanted to do, we wanted to do, and that still goes on!

TESTIMONY OF NATHAN DILWORTH

After this beautiful portrayal of Sheryl, Bradley called Nathan Dilworth to the stand. Before reporting his testimony, some explanation is needed.

Under the rules of evidence, a hostile witness and an opposing party may be called to testify and can be controlled by questions that are leading and suggestive, a technique subject to objection for other witnesses. Not only may such witnesses be led, but any effort on their part to blurt out answers that are not responsive to the question asked permits the examiner to object to the answer as "not responsive," move to have the answer stricken from the verbatim record of the testimony, and to ask that the jury be instructed to disregard it. Continued efforts can also result in a charge of direct civil contempt and an appropriate penalty by the court, either by fine or imprisonment.

Examinations requiring such close control, however, can make for dull reading. Consider this example of questioning by Mr. Post:

Q. *State your full name.*

A. *Nathan Owen Dilworth.*

Q. *Where do you live?*

A. *At Dallas, Texas.*

Q. *Lake Dallas, Texas.*

A. *No, Dallas, Texas.*

Q. *You are now 26 years old; are you not?*

A. *Yes.*

* * *

Q. *Speak right up, Mr. Dilworth. You were 22 at the time of the collision which resulted in Sheryl Bergeson's death; is that correct?*

A. *Yes, sir.*

Q. *You are a high school graduate; are you not?*

A. *Yes, sir.*

Q. *And I believe you attended high school in Oregon, true?*
A. *Yes.*
Q. *And you moved to Texas from Oregon; is that correct?*
A. *Yes, sir.*
Q. *What year?*
A. *1985.*

This method of examining produces the facts very slowly and allows the witness little or no opportunity to develop any favorable marks of character he may possess while exposing him to the duty to respond with short answers to questions accusing him of the worst possible behavior and indifference to its consequences.

In the course of discovery, as suggested earlier, statements the witness gave to his insurer and a verbatim transcript of a discovery deposition taken by Sheryl's attorneys provided the facts needed to compel him to admit conduct reported therein while allowing the examiner close control.

Depositions are transcripts of examination in the presence of counsel against and for the witness, in the presence of a legally authorized reporter, sworn to record and transcribe questions, answers, and other remarks verbatim, that is, exactly as they occur. Depositions are taken for one or more of the following reasons: 1) to find out what the witness will say; 2) to pin the witness down to a specific story; and 3) to provide a tool to impeach trial testimony with prior inconsistent statements or in efforts to deviate from a prior story at trial.

Impeach, a threatening word in any context, here means "to cast doubt on the credibility of a witness," whether in a single response or a line of testimony in a final effort to paint him an inveterate liar.

Nathan Dilworth's testimony, beyond that recorded above, will be summarized and highlighted by those occasions where inconsistencies were exposed.

Mr. Dilworth moved to Texas from Oregon in September 1985.

His father is Edward K. Dilworth, who resided in Lake Dallas. His father had not been in Wichita during the trial. He knew of no plans for his father to be in Kansas subject to a subpoena.

A subpoena is an order of the court commanding a person to appear for examination. Such orders are restricted to the jurisdictional limits of the court; in this case, the confines of the state of Kansas.

Previously, Nathan said the safety chains were attached to both the trailer and pickup at the time they left Marion and were in place at the time the vehicles came to rest after the first collision.

Q. *That's your testimony; is it, sir?*

A. *Yes, sir.*

Q. *In fact, it's your testimony, is it not, that the ball hitch came loose from the pickup just as the backhoe and the trailer turned over; is that correct?*

A. *Yes, sir.*

Up to this time, said Nathan, the ball hitch was in place, attaching the pickup to the trailer, and the safety chains were in place. He admitted hearing the testimony of Gary Thompson, the expert employed by the insurer.

He and his father came to Kansas in 1986 to perform some contracting jobs. When they left Texas, they had lined up one job at Marion and later, while here, the job at Cherryvale. His father got both jobs lined up and signed the papers on them. He denied that his father was the one who handled the business details for the contracting work. He had worked with his father "off and on" over the years. Edward Dilworth did not own all the equipment, nor was Nathan a joint owner, but they did have an agreement that the machinery would be interchangeable between the two. The money was not put in a common pot and nothing very clear about how funds were actually divided came forth. "Depended on the job and the way it was set up," but in Kansas at least each would take money from the jobs, as needed.

If ignorance is want of knowledge and stupidity its aggravated form, Nathan demonstrated its depths in his responses. Without particular antagonism, Bradley led him to admit propositions Nathan could not understand or put together in his own mind as being dangerous to his defense.

He agreed that they could have stayed in Marion that night and started their move the next day. There was plenty of time to start the next job. The decision to move that night was a joint decision, he said. Nathan could not appreciate that Bradley was fixing, little by little, the Dilworths' common legal responsibility.

And, without any reason to do so, Nathan would resist. When Bradley led with the suggestion that in their moves his father, Ed, ordinarily drove the lead vehicle, Nathan denied, *"No, sir,"* as if his very manhood was at stake. When Bradley changed to ask, *"You usually drive it?"* he was not to be trapped, answering, *"No, sir."* Trying to clarify the matter, Bradley then asked, *"Well, how do you decide who's going to drive the lead vehicle? Is it whoever is driving the Freightliner?"* Nathan thinks he is now asserting his independence by answering with another, *"No, sir,"* giving Bradley an opening to prove joint responsibility again by asking:

Q. *So it was a joint decision that night to move those vehicles in the nighttime; it that your testimony?*

A. *Yes, sir.*

Q. *It was a dark night; isn't that correct?*

A. *Yes, sir.*

Nathan knew of the condition of the pickup, the trailer brakes, and the fact he was pulling a backhoe weighing 11,500 lbs, more or less. He knew the condition of the hitch, the hazard created by "play" in the ball hitch pulling up and down. He knew all these things, as did his father, when they embarked on this nighttime journey. In short, he admitted knowing the hazards connected with the travel they had jointly undertaken.

Bradley next discussed a recorded statement taken by "one of your representatives" right after their arrival in Cherryvale. While reference was later made to the contents of that statement, the idea "your representatives" naturally suggested to the jury the presence of insurance, a topic to which plaintiff could make no direct reference.

At the time of trial, Nathan had admitted 100 percent responsibility for the collision that killed Sheryl. Until that time, both he and his father denied responsibility.

After the collision, Nathan went to Sheryl's car and heard her breathing and moaning. He had neither flares nor a flashlight that one would ordinarily expect in such an operation. A truck driver who had a flashlight stopped and attempted to warn another vehicle of the danger, but the driver was unable to stop in time and collided with the front of the pickup.

When Nathan approached Sheryl, he saw that she was seriously injured. He told her he would try to get help and that she would be all right. At that time, she turned her head toward him, looked at him, then lost consciousness. She could not answer. At this point, the truck driver came over and said, "Well, there is nothing more you can do." Shortly thereafter, the ambulance and various law enforcement agencies took over the scene and transported Sheryl to the hospital in Marion, where her death was recorded.

The night was so dark that things a hundred feet away were not visible. Regardless of the expert engineer's testimony, Nathan insisted that the impact with Sheryl's car caused the bolt and ball portion of the ball hitch to be pulled from the hole on the back bumper of the pickup and that the safety chains from the trailer to the pickup remained attached after the collision.

The Dilworths made claims for their damaged vehicles. The

pickup, for which they had paid $1,000 sometime earlier, they now claimed was worth $3,500. At first, Nathan denied making claims for damage to his pickup, but in his deposition his answer had been, "You bet I have." And even after being forced to admit that this had been his response under oath in the deposition, he thereafter reasserted his previous position that it was only his father, not he, that had made claims for damage to the pickup. Why he would regard this as important is beyond reason, but responses of this kind certainly emphasized problems of his reliability.

Nathan also knew that his father had written a threatening letter to Bradley. At this point, the jury was excused and a discussion with the judge was had concerning questioning Nathan about letters written by his father and their intended use in further questioning of Nathan. At this point, Nathan had not stated that he knew of the contents of the letters, so after lengthy argument, the court ruled that at this point the letters were not relevant. The ruling, in its practical effect, was that Bradley was precluded from pursuing that line of questioning by using the letters as a reference.

The major purpose in using the letters was rendered unnecessary when, in answer to the next questions, Nathan himself made claims that some of the people investigating the collision had been drinking liquor. He said this included the volunteer fireman and rescue crew. He said he smelled liquor on them. He had stated in his deposition that one of the officers holding the tape to take measurements at the scene smelled of alcohol.

In his deposition, Nathan had testified he was clear over to the west side of the roadway, in other words, as far as he could safely get from Sheryl's lane. He had prepared a drawing of how the vehicles came together, showing Sheryl's car hitting the trailer in his lane, the southbound lane of traffic, even though he had changed position now at trial and was admitting that his trailer hit Sheryl Bergeson's car in the northbound lane, her proper lane of travel. That drawing, identified by the court as having been drawn by Nathan, was offered into evidence. Mr. Warta stated he had no objection and the exhibit was admitted, meaning that it would go with the jury to the jury room to be considered in their deliberations.

It is difficult to imagine that any fragment of credibility remained to Nathan's character, even for things that did not matter. Like one once said, "If he touches his ear, it's okay; if he puts a finger aside his nose, okay; but when he opens his mouth. . ."

Nathan claimed Sheryl's car came sharply across and collided with the left front corner of the trailer. It lodged there and the three vehicles came south, went over into the northbound (Sheryl's) lane of travel, where it traveled up the hill to the north, the opposite of what one would expect from the physical factors where it then came to rest. Both Dilworths were present at the taking of each of their depositions, and Nathan recalled hearing his father give the same account.

Bradley asked whether Nathan had heard his father claim that Sheryl was either asleep, trying to put tapes in her tape player, or trying to commit suicide. Objection was made and sustained by Judge Theis.

Bradley then skirted the objection by getting Nathan to tell how he went to the scene the next day with a camera. He produced one picture, *Exhibit 46,* which showed an audiotape unreeled loosely along the edge of the highway in plain sight. None of the investigating officers testified to the existence of this tape for the simple reason that it was placed there shortly before the picture was taken, a not-too-bright effort to confirm a lie with a lying picture. In the formula, is a false picture worth a thousand lies?

Counsel asked permission to display this photograph to the jury, which was allowed. He also asked the judge to explain to the jury that, even though the exhibits were not all passed to the jury when they were admitted, they would be available during deliberations. The court allowed this and made comments indicating the very reason most lawyers do not like to circulate exhibits during testimony is because they distract the jury from hearing and considering the oral testimony while it is being produced. It is also likely that while viewing such evidence the jury is also distracted from allowing the exhibits the value they deserve.

Mr. Post attempted to read a portion of a letter by Ed Dilworth to Robert Laughridge of Cedar Point, driver of the vehicle that the truck driver tried unsuccessfully to flag down with his flashlight. After some argument, the court allowed these sentences to be read:

You also know your vehicle caused our vehicle to be ripped free from our trailer. The two were hooked up by the safety chain up to that time. Your vehicle in part shoved our pickup around and ripped these safety chains apart, separating the trailer from the pickup, and it was the glass, radiator fluid, and other debris from your vehicle scattered all over the crash scene that covered vital evidence to the initial accident.

Neither the Kansas Highway patrolman nor the expert hired by State Farm expressed any concern about "vital evidence being covered" by debris or radiator fluid. Probably the most maudlin reference in this letter was allowed over defendants' objection was Ed Dilworth's statement, *"You have not had to look at your vehicle mangled in your backyard."* In the context of the claim of these parents, who have had to deal with the mangled body of their dear child, the jury could hardly be expected to be aroused to anything but revulsion by such a cheap ploy.

After getting Nathan to admit that the purpose of the post-collision photo was to make it appear that Sheryl had crossed the center line and hit his vehicle, and after having him admit there were no marks on the highway to sustain this, Bradley ended direct examination.

Cross-examination by Mr. Warta is revealing principally of his aim and effort to make Nathan look like an acceptable substitute for a human with normal human relations and feelings. He was born and lived in Kalispell, Montana; Oregon, then Texas. His mother is not mentioned. He did have a father, one brother, and five sisters. He has a wife whose name is not mentioned and a child on the way. His wife was secretary to Wayne Ames, a lawyer from Texas who was also appearing as counsel for him in this case. He graduated from high school in 1982 and worked with his father and brother in a variety of employments in which he was sometimes employed as a laborer and paid an hourly wage. While he was employed by a corporation named ADA Contractors, he went on a mission for the church he belonged to, the Church of Jesus Christ of Latter Day Saints. He went to the Cleveland, Ohio, mission for 19 months. After this mission, he returned and started doing contracting, as did his father and brother. He reported that each of the three would bid jobs, the successful bidder got the proceeds and if he needed money he would get it. It was not clear if he bid the job whether his father and brother were paid. This arrangement was never made clear at any time. There was no prearranged understanding of how money was to be shared.

At this point in the trial, the hour of 4:30 p.m. had arrived, and the issue of using Ed Dilworth's letters to examine Nathan was unresolved. The court declared a recess and dismissed the jury to take up the argument on this and other legal issues which would impose liability on the senior Dilworth for actual and punitive damages.

During the course of the argument, the judge asked Bradley, "As I understand, somebody was saying when this lawsuit started that there was a $200,000 coverage and they didn't pay it. You would have settled for that amount?" After an affirmative response, the judge added, "Well, what evidence I have heard, that looks like a bad decision for the insurance company."

What should the attorney for the insurer do about comments of this kind by an experienced trial judge? He has, in effect, been told that there is probably going to be a highly unfavorable outcome to this trial if the insurer continues its defense-a prediction which came true.

Should counsel go to the claims people for the company suggesting a further effort to settle? Should these claims people concern themselves with reducing the risk of loss? Who, after all, in a mutual company bears the risk of loss? You guessed it! All the other policyholders bear the risk of premium increases necessary to cover such unjustified losses. Does this attitude of State Farm Mutual Automobile Insurance Company make it appear that it and its moral and ethical values were any better than those of its insureds, Nathan and Ed Dilworth?

One might suppose that once a verdict was rendered and judgment entered, that the insurer would pay or seek a compromise and cease incurring the expense of attorney fees, both their own and for plaintiffs, as well as the accumulation of interest, but NO! The Bergesons were to endure a paper storm of motions, appeals, and bankruptcy proceedings in Texas without ever receiving one penny except under final compulsion.

When the trial resumed, Mr. Warta continued his cross-examination of Nathan Dilworth. He covered his work experience, the move from Oregon to Texas, the acquisition of the vehicles, the pickup and the trailer. Nathan testified that he had inspected the trailer, which he had helped build. He recorded various jobs for the General Services Administration, which he had bid and completed, some with his father's help, and jobs that his father and brother bid that he helped complete. He described his work on the Marion job using the backhoe and placing rip-rap along the lakeshore to limit erosion. While on the Marion job, he stayed in a campground west of Marion. If raining, he slept in the Freightliner, otherwise in a tent. He denied any trouble with the trailer in hauling materials on the Marion job site. He reported checking the ball hitch on the bumper of the pickup, tightening it down with two pipe wrenches. He put the trailer on the hitch, hooked the safety chains to the trailer, and saw nothing wrong with it. After loading the backhoe, he discovered it was back-heavy. He and his father moved the backhoe forward on the trailer and re-fastened the back chain, and Ed brought another chain to fasten the front of the backhoe.

The project in Cherryvale was to begin the following week. The Dilworths began moving their equipment on Thursday of the preceding week.

Nathan repeated his claim that the greatest speed he reached on the trip was 45 mph and that he had no trouble with the trailer swaying or anything else out of the ordinary. He described the accident much as he had before and also the second collision involving the Laughridge car.

He also claimed to have gone to Wisconsin in the interval after the move to Cherryvale, "so he could be alone" for the two-month interval. Bradley later proved that he was in Cherryvale during this period of time, disproving even this attempt to gain sympathy.

Nathan claimed that he did not know of his father's claim for damage to the pickup and that when he discovered it, he and his father had a "big argument" and he told his father it was none of his business. He reported being very angry over his father's making this claim.

Re-direct examination followed and Bradley forced Nathan again to say, "You bet I did!" when asked if he had made claim for his damages-immediately after having denied that to the jury.

Nathan claimed to have returned from Wisconsin in November 1986. Bradley then produced records from the Corps of Engineers showing clearly that Ed and Nathan Dilworth, along with others, were listed as owners of Dilworth Construction Company working on the Corps of Engineers' project in Cherryvale.

Next, plaintiff's counsel played the tape-recorded interview between Nathan and the company representative in which he opined that Sheryl was either asleep or changing a tape in her car. Although he had claimed all along to be the owner of the pickup, in this taped telephone interview, one can hear his father Ed say that he, not Nathan, was the owner, and Nathan never refuted this claim of ownership to Mr. Conklin, the interviewer. The interview continued:

The headlights were coming south and he started waving with his flashlight at the guy, flashing the light on him, and flashing it up in the air, trying to get the guy's attention, and he's standing on the yellow line. We proceeded about 10 or 15 feet more than the Colt towards the top of the hill trying to get this guy stopped. And we started yelling at the guy and everything and he just kept coming and then he put on his brakes about 15 to 20 feet before he collided with the pickup. He hit the pickup on the left front fender with the right front fender of his car. This was maybe 200 feet from the top of the hill.

You could not see where the actual impact as related to the center line because there were no tire marks until after the impact, way past it. The first tire mark happened about 3 feet or maybe 6 feet before you see her skid marks turning and that's my trailer sideways and that's where you see me starting to straighten it out and come back into my lane.

There were no tire marks before the first impact. There's no brake marks. Even I didn't have brake marks on it.

I could not tell who was in the car as it came past. It was too dark but you know you can see figures and stuff. I'd say no, I couldn't tell clearly of what kind of person was in there or what the person was doing.

This was investigated by the highway patrol and they gave me a ticket for crossing the center line. I asked the officer at that deposition, I said, 'Now does this state I crossed the yellow line before or after?' He says, 'All it says is that you crossed the yellow line. I'm not saying before and I'm not saying after.'

And he fined me. I pleaded no contest and paid a fine on it. I sent them a check because, well, I did cross the yellow line, so, yeah, I was guilty, but if they're insinuating I did it before, you know, see it was kind of confusing.

The ball hitch popped off the nut when the trailer tipped over. It bent the ball. You can see the shaft, it's bent towards the way it tipped.

If you go straight from the end of the trailer across the road to the white line on her side, that is where I found the nut, when the trailer broke the second time. With that big, lazy jackknife it just went sideways. And then when it, when it got my car turning fast, it pulled back into my lane, you know, it kind of swung it over into my lane. And then it was tipping over and you can see the tire marks as it's tipping and it's sliding my way.

I know the ball and nut came off on the second impact when it was rolling because I was still hooked up to it, you know, when I was doing that last turn. Let me tell you the reasons why. One reason, when I looked in my mirror, I could see it back there, it was still level and still right behind the truck. Number two, if it came loose and it took off like it did, you know, 'cause that front axle on that trailer was bent to the left, that's why it took off that way, it would have took the safety chains clear off that thing and took off in the other direction and went straight down the road. And it wouldn't have took me the way it did. That's why I know it came off when it rolled.

I know that at no time before the first impact with that Colt did the trailer cross the center. I know it didn't. We never had any problem before with the hitch the way it was hooked up.

I was goin' real slow, just taking it easy. It was going good, you know, the trailer wasn't slipping or anything. I was having no problems with it.

Somebody said that the young lady had been at a PTA meeting, a parent-teacher meeting. I just found out little bits of information on it. You know, a few people talking. Every time I'd go over there to find information out from the policeman, he'd yell at me and tell me to go stand over there, just tell me to go over there. And see, what happened was about maybe an hour into his interview, he read me my rights and told me, you know I'm under arrest and all this other stuff, and he told me to go sit over there by the pickup. So I went over there and sat by the pickup.

He actually arrested me, he goes, "Nathan, I'm here to read you your rights, you're under arrest, anything you say will be held against you in a court of law." He read me all that stuff. I thought he said involuntary manslaughter, I think is what he said. He might never have said what it was for, but that's what I thought he said. He did not take me to jail. He kept me there all night long until 7:40 the next day at the scene of the accident. Then he said I'm free to go but I have to be back at the deposition.

When the accident happened, the ambulance came. They took, the first ambulance took the young girl, the second ambulance tended to those three. They told me to go wait by my car. They never even asked me if I was all right. They just told me to go sit by the car. I had nothing to drink, I don't drink, and had no drugs. I don't take drugs. I don't even take vitamins.

On the damage to the pickup, if the second car never collided with it, I wouldn't have had no damage but the bumper and about 8 inches on the fender, the back box of the pickup. When the second car came and hit, it shoved it down past the trailer and the trailer hitch cut through the fender and so that's when all the damage happened to the pickup.

I guess my father picked up the nut. I didn't. I saw it there and I pointed it out to the officer, he says, "Oh, that's not important!" I think that was some officer from Marion. The ball was still hooked to the trailer. It was still hooked to the trailer into the tongue and they took, the wrecker guy took a pry bar and it took him about 15, 20 minutes to pry that thing out of there. Until the second impact happened it shoved my, the front of the car south, well it kind of shoved the rear end towards the south, too, 'cause it went into the trailer, that's what, and it slid it down off the road, the back tires off the back of the road.

I've been driving that truck with that trailer for approximately a year, two years, with that truck. That trailer, I've been hauling that trailer with another truck for a lot longer with the same type of load. So I was familiar with it. I didn't have any problems with it. I've been pulling that trailer since way back. I used to pull it for another guy I worked for. And

I bought it off of him.

I used to pull, you know, like pickups on it, you know. He had a little Case bulldozer I used to pull with it, and I had no problem with it.

While the trial was pending, Bradley had issued a subpoena to the U.S. Army Corps of Engineers to whose employment the Dilworths' repeated reference had been made. Because of the relatively small amounts involved, the records had been hard to identify and locate, but at this time they were produced. Nathan was called to identify them, to qualify them for admission as evidence, a process called "laying a foundation" for the admission of documents.

These printed records were significant in two areas. First, they showed that Nathan's earlier testimony of going into seclusion in Wisconsin for two months because he "just wanted to be alone" was untrue and that, instead, as he had stated earlier, he went to work on the job at Cherryvale. Second, they established the continued joint venture relationship of the Dilworths in these Corps of Engineers projects, which tied together the liability of Nathan, who had admitted liability, with Edward, who did not appear and whose liability for punitive damages his insurer, State Farm, was trying to avoid.

Testimony of Edward Dilworth

Concluding plaintiff's evidence, the deposition of the senior Dilworth was read in his absence. It so closely followed his earlier statement as previously reported that it is not repeated here.

The Defense

Except for answers from Nathan Dilworth on cross-examination, after being called and recalled by Mr. Post, the defense called only one witness, Darlene Leeds. Her testimony follows.

TESTIMONY OF DARLENE K. LEEDS

Darlene K. Leeds lived at Florence, Kansas; she was 34 years old, married, with a 10-year-old son. At the time of trial, she was studying nursing at Butler County Community College, pursuing an RN status.

(As a courtesy to Mr. Warta, common in trial practice when witnesses cannot be available at other times during trial, counsel agree that a witness for the defense can be allowed to testify out of the usual order. Such was the case with Mrs. Leeds. The testimony of Nathan Dilworth was interrupted for her appearance.)

In September 1986, she worked for the City of Florence on the volunteer ambulance service. She was an American Red Cross instructor in CPR and became an EMT in February 1985. She worked with two gentlemen on the ambulance service, neither of whom were qualified to appear; one because of health problems, the other because of a serious speech impairment. So she was left to testify to the care and treatment of Sheryl. She identified the report prepared by the crew, Plaintiff's Exhibit 6. She referred to that and other documents in giving her testimony. The purpose in the defense calling her was to provide live testimony concerning the plaintiff's claim for conscious pain and suffering.

She began with the time of arrival on the scene at 10:27 that evening. She went down to the car. She checked Sheryl's pulse and found a very shallow pulse, *"about 20,"* against a normal pulse ranging from 70-100 beats per minute. She checked Sheryl's breathing and found she was getting *"about three breaths a minute"* against a normal cycle of 12-18 breaths, or respirations, per minute. Sheryl was unconscious. *"I hollered to see if she would respond, and she would not,"* Mrs. Leeds said.

The crew removed Sheryl from the car on a spine board and

started oxygen and a bag mask on her. Mrs. Leeds checked the pulse at this point and *"it was still about the same. She was getting shallower and it was getting weaker."* Respirations were still running about three a minute. Darlene Leeds attempted to insert an endotracheal tube, but it would not go in. During this time, she observed no level of consciousness at all. Sheryl made no moaning or anything.

Dr. Hodson met the ambulance. They tried CPR without success and, at the hospital, the doctor told them to stop CPR, it wasn't working. They arrived at the hospital at 10:38 p.m. It was two to three minutes thereafter that they were told to stop CPR. Dr. Hodson later recorded her death.

In cross-examination, Mr. Post established that there was no sign of life-threatening injury to Sheryl's head, nor to her lower extremities. Mrs. Leeds agreed she had no way of knowing how long Sheryl was conscious and was moaning before she arrived. There was fluid and blood in the passages required for speaking, which also prevented intubation. She did repeat that at the time she arrived, she heard labored breathing and gurgling, which she stated was caused by fluid building in Sheryl's lungs. She received notice of the EMS call at 10:17, but had no way of knowing what time the wreck had occurred or what time Edward Dilworth came in from the accident scene to report it.

Mr. Post covered more of Sheryl's injuries, the nature of hypovolemic shock, and asphyxiation associated with choking and strangling, but his principle points had been made. He defused her as an effective witness because she did not know the time Sheryl's injuries were first inflicted, the time of the collision, or the onset of the hypovolemic shock.

On re-direct, Mr. Warta had her read from the doctor's death certification that the onset between hypovolemic shock and death was "approximately 5 minutes," but neither the doctor nor the death certificate stated the interval between the trauma and the onset of hypovolemic shock. Was this to be inferred from the doctor's statement? Reason would suggest that some time interval between the trauma and the onset of shock would exist. Mrs. Leeds was not sufficiently qualified to answer that and, perhaps, counsel himself assumed that the onset of shock was immediate. At any rate, her testimony lacked that element of proof and, obviously, the jury did not attach much weight to it.

After her testimony, Mr. Warta rested, that is, concluded his defense.

(While the jury was deliberating, Nathan Dilworth, to his credit, and outside the presence of his father or anyone else, uttered two words to us during a passing encounter in the hallway. "I'm sorry.")

THE VERDICT

After a long recess while the court and counsel settled on the instructions that were given, the jury retired to begin their deliberations on the afternoon of May 2, 1990, and continued on the following day, May 3, when they concluded their findings and rendered their verdict, a copy of which follows these comments.

In answer to the two special questions, the jury found that the Dilworths were members of a business enterprise on the date of the accident and that Nathan's acts were in furtherance of that enterprise. Then it found damages to be as follows:

CONSCIOUS PAIN AND SUFFERING ....$ 100,000.00

MEDICAL EXPENSES 221.50

PECUNIARY DAMAGES 50,000.00

NON-PECUNIARY DAMAGES 250,000.00

FUNERAL EXPENSES 6,573.83

In answer to question 4, the jury also concluded that the defendants acted in a wanton manner on the date of the accident and answered "yes" to the question whether punitive damages should be assessed. It assessed those damages at $500,000.

The verdict form was signed by the jury foreman, a loan officer at an Arkansas City bank.

The jury had some inkling about the limits of non-pecuniary damages when they sent a question to the court on May 2 asking, "Is there a limit for non-pecuniary damages?" Judge Theis was visibly irritated by this question, answering it abruptly, "The jury should determine the amount of non-pecuniary damages based on the evidence and enter that figure on the verdict form."

The judgment entered by the clerk of the court is attached.

Exhibit A

AO 450 (Rev. 5/85) Judgment in a Civil Case

FILED
U.S. DISTRICT COURT
DISTRICT OF KANSAS

MAY 3 2 36 PM '90

RALPH L. DELOACH,
CLERK
BY J. Baker DEPUTY
AT WICHITA, KS.

United States District Court

DISTRICT OF KANSAS

ELDON L. BERGESON, et al

JUDGMENT IN A CIVIL CASE

V.

EDWARD K. DILWORTH and
NATHAN O. DILWORTH

CASE NUMBER: 87-1579

☒ **Jury Verdict.** This action came before the Court for a trial by jury. The issues have been tried and the jury has rendered its verdict.

☐ **Decision by Court.** This action came to trial or hearing before the Court. The issues have been tried or heard and a decision has been rendered.

IT IS ORDERED AND ADJUDGED that judgment shall be entered in favor of the plaintiff, Eldon L. Bergeson, as executor of the Estate of Sheryl Bergeson, deceased and against the defendants, Edward K. and Nathan O. Dilworth as follows:

Conscious pain and suffering		$100,000.00
Medical expenses		221.50
Pecuniary damages		50,000.00
Nonpecuniary damages	$250,000.00	
Less, amount in excess of statutory limitation pursuant to K.S.A. 60-1903(a)	150,000.00	100,000.00
Funeral expenses and monument		6,573.83
Punitive damages		500,000.00

Approved: [signature]
U.S. District Judge

May 3, 1990
Date

RALPH L. DE LOACH
Clerk

ENTERED ON THE DOCKET
DATE: 05-03-90

[signature]
(By) Deputy Clerk Anne Butler

10

JUDGMENT

When a civil action results in damages allowed by a jury verdict, a document called Judgment in a Civil Action is entered by the judge presiding, or in his absence at the time, by another judge of the district court who reviews the file, including the verdict, then signs and files it with the clerk. It is interesting to note that while Judge Theis was involved with other orders entered, the judgment in this case was signed by the Honorable Wesley Brown.

If nothing is done at that point, that is, unless the judgment debtor comes forward and pays voluntarily, something must be done to enforce payment. One common procedure is for the plaintiff to file an Affidavit of Garnishment, which asks the court on the facts to issue its order against the party responsible and having the assets to pay the judgment into court to be paid out to the plaintiffs.

Interestingly, the verb "garnish," like many English words, has more than one meaning. Its first meaning according to Merriam Webster is "to decorate, embellish," but under its kindred noun "garnishment," it is defined as "a legal summons or warning concerning the attachment of property to satisfy a creditor." An Order of Garnishment is issued by the clerk of the court and, as directed in the affidavit, served by a process server on the party named. As stated before, State Farm Mutual Automobile Insurance Company had issued its indemnity policy to the Dilworths in which it agreed to "indemnify" them against any such judgment. Indemnify in this sense means "to pay." Since this company had the contractual duty to pay, it was named as "garnishee," the one against whom an order of garnishment is issued.

Even before this order was issued, State Farm asked the court for permission to pay in the $200,000 policy limits, apparently inspired by the claim committee's notion that State Farm was not responsible for any excess beyond this amount, disregarding the line of Kansas cases well known, at least to its attorneys, that the company might just be compelled to pay the entire judgment as we will discuss further. Obviously, if the money is collected and the only appeal involves the amount or seeking to reduce it, the fact that it has already been collected renders an appeal meaningless, and an appellate court will not waste time deciding what might have been. It is called a "moot" issue, meaning any attempt to decide the issue would be meaningless.

A supersedeas bond would require that the party obligated to pay would find some other financially responsible party having assets sufficient to pay such judgment, called a "surety," who would sign a bond, agreeing to pay the judgment determined by the appellate court if the appeal fails, the judgment below is approved, or, in legal parlance, affirmed. If the appeal is successful and the judgment is vacated and a new trial granted, the surety has no further duty to pay.

Of course, because of the risk involved, a surety would demand payment. In this case, the premium for a surety bond would likely be equal to the judgment itself. The bond must provide that the principal (State Farm) and the surety would agree to pay 125% of the judgment. For example, a $10,000 judgment would require a bond of $12,500 plus the agreement to pay all interest accruing on the judgment and the costs taxed by the court to cover its administrative expenses. Again, this obligation to pay comes about only if the original judgment is approved or affirmed by the appellate court.

What Were They Thinking?

While we were investigating the claim, researching the legal questions, and involved in preparing the case for trial, State Farm and its claims people were considering their responses. In the process called "discovery," in which each adverse party must respond to requests of the other for relevant evidence and clues that might lead to the discovery of relevant evidence, State Farm produced reports of its claims committee, memos, and correspondence of claims people, and boxes of other information pertaining to these claims.

When the journal entry of judgment was filed, granting judgment to Sheryl's parents, including her estate, State Farm attempted (for reasons not all together clear) to pay the $200,000 policy limits into court, trying to take the position that this would be the extent of the company's liability for that judgment. Bradley had, in the meantime, filed garnishment proceedings, called "Garnishment in Aid of Execution," which is just another way of trying to collect the money that the jury awarded, reduced by some statutory limitations.

While this was afloat, State Farm filed a separate action in the state court in a proceeding called a "declaratory judgment" action, a remedy in which a party in a defensive position can ask the court to define its rights and obligations. The state court judge, knowing that the federal district court had jurisdiction of the underlying case, refused to consider any such action, but this was one of many "tricks" State Farm pulled, trying to escape liability and the bulldog pursuit by Bradley Post to collect the judgment.

Once a judgment is entered, even if the liability is determined, a party has a right to appeal to the court of appeals in the proper circuit. However, the judgment creditor can proceed with efforts to collect during the appeal and, if successful, would render an appeal hearing fruitless. The law provides that the appealing party may stay, or stop, the proceedings to collect by filing what is called a supersedeas bond for 125% of the judgment, interest, and costs, having the effect of guaranteeing payment of the judgment by another responsible party, called a surety, if the judgment is affirmed, that is, approved by the appellate court.

State Farm's liability under the circumstances of this case was not limited by the amount of the policy as already mentioned, for the law provides that the insurance company must give the interests of its insured the same consideration it gives to its own interests in choosing to settle the case. By offering its policy amount of $200,000 before a lawsuit was filed, it could have avoided any further liability on its part, leaving the Bergesons to rely on the availability of other collectible assets of the Dilworths. They, being without assets beyond what are exempt under the law, would not have been worth pursuing and the clients would have had no choice but to accept the $200,000 in payment of their claims. Foolishly, the company never made such a choice and thus rendered itself liable for any amount finally adjudged to be due.

Given State Farm's continued efforts to avoid bonding the appeal, Bradley was inspired to look again at the terms of the insurance policy to see what the company's obligation was at this point. He relates the experience as almost a divine encounter. While walking to the YMCA to exercise by doing laps in the indoor pool, it struck him that the policy includes such a provision. By this time, the Dilworths had filed for bankruptcy in the Eastern District of Texas, and we had retained counsel in Texas to advise us.

Under the "Supplementary Payments," the State Farm policy provided, as follows:

The company will pay, in addition to the applicable limit of liability. . . (b) *premiums on appeal bonds required in any such suit . . . but the company shall have no obligation to apply for or furnish any such bonds.*

If, under the coverage afforded by the policy of insurance, the company was obligated to pay the cost of a supersedeas bond in order to maintain its appeal, this meant that there was no "judgment for excess above the applicable limits," the stated limits having been extended by the supplemental payment provisions.

Bradley's opinion was confirmed in the ISO (Insurance Services Organization), which prints advisory information construing policy terms for insurance agents' use in advising their customers. On this identical provision, the manual provided:

In this section, the insurer is agreeing to pay for appeal bonds which guarantee the payment of a judgment in the case of an unsuccessful appeal.

We informed the attorney we had employed in Dallas, whom we considered an expert in the field of our contention. He confidently assured us that there was no way we could force the insurer to pay for such a bond. With pleasure, we retained for the client his letter congratulating us "on forcing State Farm to bond the entire judgment."

By letter of April 25, 1991, our friend Larry Withers, now also representing State Farm, informed us that Fidelity & Deposit Company of Maryland had issued its bond securing the judgment and stopping further garnishment proceedings during appeal, the bond being in the amount of $945,994.16, which assured the Bergesons that if State Farm's appeal to the 10th Circuit Court of Appeals failed, Fidelity & Casualty Company would be on the hook to see that this amount was paid to our clients.

CLAIM COMMITTEE REPORT

In its claims department structure, State Farm maintains a claim committee whose job it is to review claims, give its opinion of the extent of the risk of exposure to damages of a dollar amount, based on all the factors that go into the mix of litigation and, if indicated, recommend settlement and the amount that should be offered.

Five men from the claim department evaluated the case and concluded that the death claim was worth $65,000. The report notes that when the statement of Mrs. Koslowski was obtained, the Bergesons had moved to amend to claim punitive damages, which was allowed. They then reported that they were advised that if punitive damages were allowed, they would probably not exceed $75,000. They note that in response to their offer of $65,000, the plaintiffs had refused and demanded the policy limits of $200,000, and, in addition, their insureds, the Dilworths, demanded they pay the policy limits or be held responsible for the excess judgment. The recommendation of the claim superintendent, John Hoke, was to offer to settle the claim up to $125,000. (This last amount was never offered!) The claim committee report includes this recital:

The law in Kansas is very clear. Punitive damages are not payable under the terms of a liability policy in Kansas. The law in Kansas holds that payment of punitive damages is against public policy.

The Law the Claim Committee Did Not Include

The claim committee failed to take into account a well-developed area of the law in Kansas that provides: 1) the insurer, State Farm in this case, had a duty to consider the interest of its insured, Ed Dilworth, as fairly and fully as its own interest; 2) where the case could be settled by paying its policy limits of $200,000 and it failed to do so; and 3) where its insured had demanded payment of its policy limits; 4) the company could be held liable for any judgment in excess of this amount; 5) including punitive damages.

Whether this was not reported by the attorneys representing State Farm or whether the probability of any excess seemed so remote as not to raise the need to discuss that provision of the law, it was not done and for that and other reasons, only the $65,000 offer was ever made.

The claim committee report concluded:

It should be noted that neither of our defense counsel place a value on the death claim in excess of $65,000 for general damages.

There is no evidence of bad faith in our handling, and we should not be, regardless of plaintiff's contentions, held guilty of same.

Proceed with a declaratory action on the issue of punitive damages, and be guided accordingly, pending the result.

The jury that was not expected to render a verdict in excess of $65,000, in fact rendered a verdict of $906,795.33, which was reduced to $756,795.33 because the Kansas legislature by statute limited recovery of non-pecuniary damages to $100,000 and this limit could not be disclosed to the jury.

In a re-hearing claim committee report, the attorney recommended an appeal to the 10th Circuit and to tender the

$200,000 policy limits into court. The narrative detail in the report consisted of the usual self-justification detail without any showing of remorse for so badly misjudging the culpability of its insureds, and the remarkable personality of the girl who was killed. Their ignorance continued to display its brass by this statement:

We will pay our limits of $200,000 to the clerk of the federal court, which will stop the interest on the judgment of $756,795.33.

This was another not so erudite statement that did not work out in practice, as we explain later.

On May 17, 1990, two weeks after the entry of judgment, the defendants filed a motion and memorandum to amend the judgment by remittitur, legalese for reduction. The gist of this motion was that the Bergesons had asked only $250,000 in punitive damages and the jury doubled that request to $500,000, so, according to defendant's thinking, the judge should knock $250,000 off the judgment entered.

Before that matter could be resolved, State Farm, under the name of the Dilworths, filed a notice of appeal and a motion for court approval of a deposit of funds, which we will take up hereafter.

Plaintiffs filed an objection to the motion for remittitur, accompanied by a memorandum discussing the issue presented: whether the jury was free to award more than the plaintiffs had asked, and whether, considering the facts of the case, the court could approve the punitive award as reasonable.

The court considered the motion for remittitur and the motion that State Farm be permitted to pay in its $200,000 claiming that this represented the limits of its liability, that this could be drawn down by the Bergesons if it was in satisfaction of the entire judgment or, that it be invested by the clerk pending the appeal.

The motion imposed the further condition that it was tendered only as to the actual damage portion of the judgment; it was not to be taken as any agreement with the judgment, nor considered as an abandonment or impairment in any way of their right of appeal. In short, what the defendants offered at the front, they took away by their conditions at the rear.

Timely objections were made by attorneys for the Bergesons, and on May 25, 1990, the court ruled on both motions. Regarding the jury award of punitive damages, the court ruled that whether to award such damages and the amount thereof was for the jury to determine. As to the reasonableness of the amount (which the court must decide), the judge recited the awful conduct of these defendants and found the amount reasonable and overruled the motion on that issue.

Considering the request to deposit funds, the court, noting the Federal Rules of Civil Procedure, and the fact that the defendants did not intend to move for a stay of execution pending the appeal, denied the request to deposit funds with the clerk.

Before this order was entered, the Bergesons requested the issuance of an order of garnishment, as previously stated. "To garner" is to gather in, as in a harvest. The Bergesons desired to begin the harvest, as quickly as possible. State Farm, the garnishee, filed its verified answer on June 14, 1990, stating that it had not delivered anything to the Dilworths, that it had issued a liability insurance policy with limits of $200,000, that it was not liable for any amounts above, and that the punitive damage award was not its responsibility. It included other window dressing to persuade its other claims people that the company was being cruelly used and misjudged.

Counsel for Bergesons filed a reply to the garnishee's answer, as authorized by Kansas statutes, reciting the history of the case, the deceptive practices of State Farm in failing to negotiate in good faith, breaching the duty that it had to the Dilworths (as fiduciaries for them) being in a position of trust and confidence to keep them informed of their rights in insisting that the case be settled within the policy limits. We then asked that the court determine that State Farm owed the entire judgment and that it be ordered to pay in the $200,000 to be drawn down and for other relief.

Bradley then began aggressive actions in the form of various discovery procedures to secure from the mouth of the Dilworths and from the records and statements of claim department personnel the facts to support the claim of bad faith, unfair dealing, and the breach of fiduciary duty it owed the Dilworths. These included interrogatories (questions), requests for admissions, and requests for production of documents from State Farm as well as both Nathan and Edward Dilworth. These were followed by notices to take depositions of the Dilworths and a number of claims representatives of State Farm.

Bankruptcy

All of these proceedings were interrupted when on June 27, 1990, Nathan Dilworth filed a voluntary petition in bankruptcy in the Eastern District of Texas sitting at Sherman, Texas. The same day, Ed Dilworth and his wife, Margaret Ann Dilworth, also filed a voluntary petition in the same court. The significance of this is the "automatic stay," which figures prominently in the proceedings thereafter.

The automatic stay says "don't!" to anyone trying to enforce any judgment against the debtors or their property by trying to obtain possession of the property of the bankrupt's estate; or the debtors themselves to create, perfect, or enforce liens against property of the estates of the debtors; or to collect, assess, or recover a pre-petition claim against the debtors or claim a setoff to pre-petition debts owing to the debtors. In short, to do nothing except preserve the status quo as it existed immediately before the filing of the bankruptcy petitions.

The automatic stay took center stage in another maneuver by State Farm, the Dilworths, and their personal lawyer, Wayne Ames. Lifting the stay in order to proceed with garnishment of State Farm's assets began the foray, followed by Ames' false and groundless accusation that Bradley Post and Don Shultz had violated the automatic stay. Then Ames sought to lift the stay so that State Farm could continue to pursue its appeal to the 10th Circuit while holding the Bergesons at bay from either collecting their judgment or forcing State Farm to post a supersedeas bond. All these we will look at up close.

MOTION BY ELDON BERGESON TO LIFT THE STAY

On July 16, 1990, Eldon's motion was received and filed in the clerk's office in Texas. There were two estates: Ed's and Nathan's, so that every pleading had to be filed in each. The motion recited the basic facts of the Dilworths' actions in causing Sheryl's death, the recovery of a judgment, the coverage afforded by State Farm, the pendency of the appeal, and the pendency of the garnishment. Far from doing anything against the interests of the debtors, the motion set out the benefit that would accrue to the bankrupts and their estates if Eldon were permitted to proceed with the two-fold aim of forcing State Farm by garnishment to pay the judgment, or, as it was obligated to do under the supplemental payments provisions of its policy, to provide a supersedeas bond in the appeal.

Ames filed his objection to Eldon's motion to lift the stay, claiming that Bergesons wished "to proceed with a garnishment action and an additional count of bad faith against State Farm Mutual Insurance Company and Nathan Owen Dilworth" and Edward Kay and Margaret Dilworth. Whether Mr. Ames even understood that the claim of bad faith and breach of fiduciary duties we were making was charged only against State Farm for failing in its legal, contractual obligations to his clients, the Dilworths, we never knew, even though he had many times been informed in detail of our position. It appears rather that he was willing to state anything even if he knew it to be false to help State Farm in its dilatory practices against the Bergesons and incidentally against the interests of his own clients, the Dilworths.

On September 7, 1990, the Honorable C. Houston Abel, presiding judge, granted Mr. Bergeson's motion, lifting the automatic stay and adding, "The Trustee, Linda Payne and movant, Eldon L. Bergeson, are authorized to pursue and proceed with the garnishment action pending in the federal district court in the state of Kansas." It is appropriate to mention also in his findings he concluded, "It is in the best interest of the debtors' estates that the stay be lifted so that the trustee and the movant can proceed with the garnishment action in Kansas against State Farm to pursue all amounts due the parties under the civil judgment rendered against the debtor." Whether or not Mr. Ames ever understood that we were looking only to State Farm to pay, the judge obviously did.

On August 10, 1990, State Farm had also filed its lock-step objection to Eldon's motion to lift the stay, and although its arguments were somewhat more sophisticated than that of Mr. Ames, the court made no reference to its arguments in his order. One almost had the sense that, while State Farm's attorneys were probably amused at Mr. Ames' arguments, they continued to believe his assistance was of value. Whether they paid him for these antics, we are not aware. A substantial bill for services and expenses for trial testimony and other expenses was sent to State Farm by the Dilworths. The fees and expenses they claimed also included amounts they had paid to Mr. Ames, but the payment to them by State Farm excluded the amounts the Dilworths had paid to attorney Ames. We still believed it possible that State Farm may have paid Mr. Ames indirectly for some of his services in connection with the case or through some other benefit, but we did not receive documents showing any bill or payment.

MR. AMES' PURSUIT OF SANCTIONS

On August 8, 1990, Mr. Ames filed a motion for contempt, requesting sanctions for violation of the automatic stay. To its credit, State Farm did not join in this motion. To demonstrate how far off the mark Mr. Ames appeared to be throughout these proceedings, he began his motion by stating "that Eldon L. Bergeson, respondent, acting by and through his attorneys of record . . . is in contempt for violation of the automatic stay" and requests sanctions of "civil or criminal contempt" penalties. Obviously, he was asking that Eldon Bergeson be found in contempt for some conduct of his attorneys. How the client could be found in contempt for conduct of his attorneys, he never explains. The acts claimed as constituting contempt and violations of the stay included:

> *His attorneys . . . have nevertheless continued full steam ahead in their purported garnishment by Bradley Post who has filed a response in the Kansas court to the plea in abatement and . . . has issued or re-issued notice of intent to take depositions and other actions . . . in an attempt to position respondent [presumably Eldon] more favorably as a judgment creditor and . . . in a wilful, deliberate, and contumacious disregard of the exclusive jurisdiction of this honorable court.*
>
> *Donald Shultz has filed his motion for oral argument on such motions as have been filed . . . and has likewise acted in a wilful, deliberate, and contumacious manner, ...*

We, of course, immediately filed our written defenses to the false and groundless claims, observing that Ames, in an apparent attempt to trick us into disregarding the automatic stay, had filed a totally superfluous motion entitled, "A Plea in Abatement," in which he asked the district court to do what the automatic stay would do simply upon filing of the bankruptcy petitions. We had filed a response to that "plea" admitting the effectiveness of the automatic stay and promising to file a motion to lift that stay "in the near future." All of the other actions he complained of were done before the petitions were filed, except that under a court rule, motions not objected to within 10 days are deemed granted. While recognizing the validity of the automatic stay, we filed our response, which had the effect of Ames and State Farm gaining an unfair advantage against Eldon Bergeson. We believe and set out in our response that this was a concerted effort by Ames and State Farm to use the stay as a sword instead of a shield, to delay proceedings in accord with State Farm's stated policy in regard to appeal bonds, and deny a remedy to the plaintiffs. Ames would later ask, without success, to withdraw and dismiss what he must have recognized was dangerous for him.

On September 4, 1990, two motions were filed with the clerk in bankruptcy. The first was our motion to impose sanctions under Rule 9011 in bankruptcy, the very thing Mr. Ames came to realize as the danger of filing false and defamatory actions for sanctions against Eldon Bergeson's attorneys, which we will discuss later. The second was a motion by the Dilworths, strange as it may seem in light of their vociferous objections to Eldon's motion, to lift the automatic stay. However, the difference in their motion and Eldon's lay in the content of these motions.

Eldon Bergeson's motion was to lift the stay so that matters might proceed in the district court as well as in the court of appeals. Ames' motions for the Dilworths contained these limiting elements (remembering that on this date the court had not heard or granted the Bergeson motion):

1) The motion asked for lifting the stay "so as to permit movant . . . to proceed with his appeal . . . to United States Court of Appeals . . .

> 2) Debtor cannot proceed with the filing of a brief in the appeal unless a relief from automatic stay is granted.
>
> 3) Debtor seeks discharge of the judgment, but disputes the . . . figure in fairness to all creditors . . . .
>
> 4) Debtor would also show that the judgment creditor continues to attempt full payment by way of garnishment proceedings . . . and unless he is allowed to continue the appeal, his rights as debtor will be severely jeopardized.

The tenor of the motion, without being open enough to say so, is asking the court to relieve the Dilworths of the restraints of the stay but to leave it in place against Mr. Bergeson and his parties in interest. Appended to the Dilworths' motion is a copy of the judgment in the district court and a notice from the court of appeals stating that the Dilworth motion, there to extend the time for filing a brief to 35 days, is granted provisionally, or if no brief is filed to advise the court of the status in bankruptcy as regards the lifting of the stay.

Our Response

Our response to this motion set forth numerous reasons running to the total falsity of the claimed relationship of the Dilworths, including their right of standing to file such a motion, the false claim that State Farm was a creditor of the Dilworths, that the Bergeson plaintiffs were creditors of the estate seeking compensation from the bankrupts, and so forth. The details of that response so demonstrate the falsity of Mr. Ames and the Dilworths and the real reasons behind these dodges:

1) The motion should be denied until State Farm posted a supersedeas bond or paid the premium for such a bond in accordance with its insurance contract.

2) The Dilworths have no standing to process an appeal since the trustee in bankruptcy takes charge of all assets as an attaching creditor, and the trustee filed no such motion, or State Farm as insurer, since it was now obligated to pay the entire judgment, and State Farm had filed no motion to lift the stay to continue the appeal.

3) After the trial, State Farm filed a motion for remittitur to reduce the judgment, followed by a motion to pay its policy limits ($200,000) into court, as against the amount required to stay the enforcement of the judgment pending appeal, to wit: $945,994.16.

4) Mr. Post repeatedly informed Mr. Ames and attempted to telephone him, advising of State Farm's obligation to bond the appeal, which would relieve the Dilworths of any proceedings against them.

5) State Farm had adopted a policy as set out in its claims practice manual of using dilatory tactics to avoid bonding the appeal.

6) The Dilworths' request, again without standing, since such action would be up to the trustee, to have the Bergeson judgment discharged. (No explanation how it would be in the Dilworths' interest to discharge the debt and still continue the appeal.)

7) Assets of the debtors' estates should not be used to pursue the appeal and, if State Farm was paying for the appeal, then it is the proper party to seek relief from the stay.

8) The debtors state, as a conclusion, that their inability to pursue the appeal would jeopardize their rights as debtors. This conclusion is not justified and as already stated, for numerous reasons, the Dilworths were not debtors of the Bergesons, neither was the trustee, as guardian of their estates.

9) If State Farm were compelled to pay the judgment, the debtors' estates could only benefit.

Appended to this response were:

1) a copy of Judge Theis's order denying the motion for remittitur;

2) a face sheet and supplemental payment provisions of State Farm's insurance contract providing for payment of a bond pending appeal;

3) an affidavit of Bradley Post setting out in detail the actions of State Farm in attempts to avoid spending any money;

4) a copy of State Farm's 1972 "Excess Liability Handbook," including:

> *3b. We may be in a position to use dilatory procedure in a garnishment, pending outcome of the appeal.*

5) the affidavit continued, listing the efforts set out above, including the notion that State Farm desired to pay its proceeds into the bankruptcy (still the province only of the trustee), employing an attorney, listing State Farm as a creditor (although neither in the schedules or under oath at the First Meeting of Creditors was there any claim that State Farm owed them any money);

6) State Farm itself even filed an objection to Eldon Bergeson's motion to lift the stay, in keeping with the dilatory practices section of its handbook.

In all this warfare concerning the automatic stay, one refreshing reply was filed by an attorney for State Farm indicating that not everyone was corrupted by the State Farm touch. Attorney Richard G. Dafoe of a firm in Dallas, Texas, filed a reply to Mr. Ames' motion for relief from automatic stay and in it revealed himself to be a person of integrity and professional ethics. While we disagreed with regard to some legal opinions and conclusions, he honestly and forthrightly stated a credible position. He recited the facts of the insurance coverage and the judgment, the fact that the Dilworths appealed, and the order previously mentioned concerning the filing of a brief or lifting the stay. He correctly stated that State Farm was not a party to the action, which is true in that the insurer in Kansas is to indemnify its insured and provide it a defense. Only the insured is named in the lawsuit.

We disagreed with his opinion whether State Farm had standing to appeal and whether State Farm had an obligation to bond the appeal. Not being familiar with Kansas law, Mr. Dafoe was doubtless unaware of the provisions that require the insurer to deal honestly and fairly, giving equal regard to the interests of the insured as it does to its own interests and, if it fails to do so, it becomes liable for the entire judgment, as here. He admits that the insurance policy is not an asset of the bankrupt estates and the trustee was <u>not</u> administering the underlying lawsuit or the insurance policy.

One of the outstanding things he admits for his client in his response:

There is no benefit to this estate in postponing or deferring a lifting of the stay to allow the debtors to pursue an appeal. There is no basis for the trustee opposing the appeal, and the administration of the estate would not be affected by the appeal. The appeal record is established and the debtors would have no substantial involvement in the appeal. From all appearances, this is a no-asset bankruptcy case and, thus, the only proceeds that Bergeson can hope to recover are proceeds on the insurance policy.

At any rate, it was refreshing after our dealings with State Farm in Kansas and with Mr. Ames' wallowing to encounter Mr. Dafoe's refreshing good character.

MOTION FOR SANCTIONS AGAINST WAYNE B. AMES

On September 4, 1990, Eldon L. Bergeson, through his attorneys, filed a motion for sanctions, requesting that sanctions, attorney fees, and expenses be imposed against Mr. Ames based on his false accusations mentioned earlier. Sanctions would include a fine or penalty imposed by the court. At a hearing in our defense, we were told by the court that the minimum fine he imposed was $5,000. The allowance of attorney fees and expenses would free Mr. Bergeson from paying the fees and expenses in preparing pleadings, appearing at Tyler, Texas, and the travel and other attendant expenses. On September 28, under cover of a letter dated September 24, 1990, Mr. Ames filed a notice in both cases withdrawing his motion for sanctions, accompanied by an order dismissing his motion for sanctions, stating in his notice only that "he no longer desires to pursue said motion." But, before deciding to withdraw and dismiss his motion, he had obtained a hearing date of August 14, 1990, at Sherman, Texas. Because Mr. Post was returning from out of state at that time, it was necessary to employ an attorney in Texas in our behalf to be sure Mr. Ames was unable to have his motion granted and, out of concern, Mr. Post made arrangements to be in Sherman on the hearing date. Of course, no action was taken on Mr. Ames' motion, but his actions in filing the accusations was sufficient to form the basis for a contempt proceeding against him.

Bankruptcy Rule 9011, in relevant part, provides:

The signature of an attorney . . . constitutes a certificate by him that he has read the document; that to the best of his knowledge, information, and <u>belief, formed after reasonable inquiry</u>, it is well grounded in fact and ... that it <u>is not interposed for any improper purpose, such as to harass, to cause delay, or to increase the cost of litigation</u>.

The rule authorizes imposition of "an appropriate sanction," which may include attorney fees and expenses incurred because of the filing of the document.

The statements included in the documents Mr. Ames signed and filed were false and known to him to be false, seeing that he had received copies of all our pleadings, in each of which we recognized the effectiveness of the stay order and honored it. Knowing that his pleading was not at all grounded in fact, the only purpose for filing and pursuing it was to harass, delay, and increase the cost of litigation. Having the record of State Farm's rule for avoiding having to provide a supersedeas bond pending appeal, it is most likely that Mr. Ames' purpose was to ingratiate himself with State Farm and to collect fees for his conduct.

Not surprisingly, an inquiry into his standing with the State Bar of Texas revealed the following:

- *A reprimand on April 4, 1968;*
- *Suspension on October 24, 1972, for a 7-year probated sentence assessed in the 104th Judicial District Court;*
- *Held in contempt on February 25, 1974, by the 168th Judicial District, including a $500 fine and jail sentence;*
- *October 14, 1974, he resigned in lieu of disciplinary proceedings before the Supreme Court of Texas;*
- *Reinstatement to the practice on January 28, 1980, by the 199th Judicial District Court; and*
- *At the date of the report, July 6, 1990, a member in good standing.*

This information in the form of a letter from the State Bar of Texas was attached to Mr. Post's affidavit.

On August 27, 1992, the Honorable Houston Abel imposed sanctions totaling $6,766 against this luminary of the Texas bar for attorney fees and expenses. Proof of the esteem in which he was held by his countrymen came when he lacked funds to pay this small sum and it went forever unpaid. Fortunately for Texas and the world, his kind are usually run to ground and may finish without assets. It also serves to illustrate the saying, "Ignorance of the law is no excuse, except for lawyers."

THE 10TH CIRCUIT APPEAL

Every party to a lawsuit has the right to appeal and review by a higher court. In the federal system, the initial appeal is to a circuit court that hears appeals from a number of district courts within a geographic area. Usually, this ends the chain of appeals in civil cases. The appeal hearing and ruling itself is preceded with a series of pleadings of little significance to the issues involved. Matters get started seriously when the aggrieved party, called the "appellant," files his "brief" in which he informs the court of his complaint, and why he thinks he was wronged, and gives a brief statement of the facts and the law he believes entitles him to some relief from the judgment in the trial court. The ultimate measure of the quality of workmanship in a brief is usually measured by the decision by the appellate judges, but not always. Like the weather, a dull day is often heralded by a bright morning, and a poor brief may be all that is needed when an injustice is clear.

But, to the work! In this case, the appeal was taken alleging errors by a highly respected trial judge to a panel of three judges who are appointed for life, who are not moved by mere rhetoric such as was displayed in the appellant's brief. The Dilworths had three complaints: 1) the admission into evidence of Ed Dilworth's letters addressed to Bradley Post and to Robert Laughridge; 2) the jury instructions concerning what was required to include Ed Dilworth in the verdict for punitive damages; and 3) the defendants were legally entitled to a new trial on all issues.

The brief itself consisted of 25 pages of letter-size paper bound with plastic binders and accompanied by an addendum of exhibits consisting of 13 pages similarly bound and containing copies of the exhibits from the trial to allow the court easy reference to those keyed to their arguments. Following a statement of the issues, the brief next sets out the facts the appellant relies on in support of the issues raised, and then the legal arguments, together with the references to cases and legal treatises applying the law to the facts, real or imagined. Apart from copying the briefs in full, we can only comment briefly on what we regard as mistakes by the appellants, the Dilworths.

The first issue reads:

The District Court erred in admitting into evidence letters containing untrue, prejudicial, and inflammatory statements written by defendant Edward K. Dilworth many months after the accident.

Ordinarily an issue raised in an appellant's brief needs to be couched in terms that coincide as precisely as possible with the legal principle involved. Here, the real legal issue was whether under the federal rules of evidence, rules which apply in federal trials (to the exclusion of state rules), these letters should have been seen by the jury. Couched in legal terms, the issue would be stated:

Did the District court abuse its discretion in admitting into evidence letters written months after the accident?

In its written decision, the court of appeals followed this path:

1) the Federal Rules of Evidence apply; 2) all evidence which tends to make a material fact more or less probable is admissible; 3) even relevant evidence may be excluded if its value is substantially outweighed by the danger of unfair prejudice; and finally, 4) even if the trial court abuses its discretion, when the error does not affect a substantial right of the party claiming error, the judgment will not be reversed. The court carefully reviewed the evidence along the lines it set out and concluded that Judge Theis had not abused his discretion.

On the next issue, questioning the court's instructions on whether Edward Dilworth could be found liable for punitive damages merely because he and Nathan were partners, the court carefully compared the instructions given to the jury and the evidence bearing on Edward's guilty knowledge of the trailer without brakes, a defective ball hitch, the fact that Edward claimed to have observed the pickup and trailer in progress in his rear-view mirror only 50 feet in front of Nathan, and concluded,

"We do not believe that the particular language to which he [Edward] points us misled the jury in such a manner as to require reversal." In fact, the court found "if anything, the instructions were more deferential to defendants than was required, as the jury was instructed that it must find both wanton conduct by Edward and a business enterprise in order to find him liable for punitive damages."

Another basis for evaluating any brief is the court's use or rejection of cases cited therein. In one case referred to as O'Gilvie, the court found it turned on another issue and "does not stand for the broad proposition" to which Dilworths were trying to apply it. Another case cited by them, Ettus v. Orkin Exterminating Co., applied state law on the evidentiary question which was guided here only by federal law, saying, "We do not read ADHS for the broad proposition argued by defendants." In other words, it had no application.

By contrast, of the cases cited in the brief filed for the Bergesons, called "appellees," the court cited six of them in its opinion as being applicable to the legal issues involved. Remembering that these judges have their own law clerks to assist in doing legal research to locate applicable cases, it is reassuring to have so many cases argued by us adopted by the court in its opinion.

Needless to say, on March 30, 1992, the 10th Circuit Court of Appeals affirmed the judgement of the trial court, the three-judge panel being Holloway, Ballock, and Teth, with Justice Ballock entering the order.

The Declaratory Judgment Action

The principal litigation in the United State District Court was already over two years old when State Farm Mutual Automobile Insurance Company brought us to battle on yet another front. On January 22, 1990, it filed a petition in state court in Sedgwick County for declaratory judgment against its own insureds, Edward K. Dilworth and Nathan O. Dilworth, and included Eldon L. Bergeson, both as an individual and in his representative capacity. In its petition, State Farm recited its policy coverage as indemnitors for the Dilworths and reported first that Eldon had been granted permission by the federal court to amend to claim punitive damages. The heart of the allegations was that State Farm disclaimed any liability coverage under its policy because the public policy of the state of Kansas prohibited responsibility for such damages. This skirted the truth. Without including Eldon's reasons for claiming that such coverage was afforded under the circumstances of this case, State Farm made the necessary threshold claim for declaratory judgment and ended its petition with a prayer, finding that punitive damages were not afforded coverage under its policy.

The federal court order granting Eldon's motion to amend to claim punitive damages was entered on August 22, 1989. The basis for our motion and the order allowing amendment to claim punitive damages was not based on any change in the public policy of the state of Kansas, which was that the standard automobile indemnity policy afforded no coverage for such damages where extenuating circumstances did not exist. To the contrary, the order of the federal court allowing us to proceed on our punitive damage claim was based not only on the gross and wanton conduct of their own insureds, but also upon the bad faith and unfair dealing of State Farm, and upon its breach of fiduciary duty owed to both its insureds and to Sheryl Bergeson and her estate, which was at the same time also insured by State Farm. None of this was referenced in their petition to the state court, although these claims were well known to them.

Kansas law provided that, with respect to its stated policy limits, in this case $200,000, the insurer had a duty to use good faith to its insureds in seeking to settle the case before suit was instituted. In this determination, the insurer was to give the interests of its insureds the same consideration it gave its own interests. Also, while knowing that it insured Sheryl Bergeson, as well as the Dilworths, a fiduciary duty was owed Sheryl and Eldon, as her successor in interest, to keep them fully informed as to the developments in the investigation.

Without notifying Eldon of such fact, State Farm employed an accident reconstruction expert to investigate and report his findings. The results of this investigation were that the Dilworths' attempts to blame Sheryl for causing her own death were false and that, in fact, the collision was a result of their negligence. This report was withheld from Eldon and his representatives until State Farm was compelled to disclose it, long after the company knew its contents, under the federal discovery rules. We also believed this report was withheld from their insureds and prevented their making a demand for State Farm to pay its policy limits, which plaintiffs had previously offered to accept in full settlement.

Also, on April 4, 1989, their adjuster took a statement from Mrs. Koslowski which revealed that the injuries and death of Sheryl were the result of the gross and wanton conduct of the Dilworths.

In our answer to State Farm's petition, we set out the fiduciary obligation that extended to our clients because State Farm insured

Sheryl, as well as the Dilworths, and the breach of that duty by State Farm and its refusal to settle with us for the $200,000 policy limits, which we had offered to accept. We also referred to the fact, based on its failure to keep the Dilworths informed, that they may have demanded State Farm pay its policy limits, a situation borne out by later discovery. We also indicated our belief that "any reasonable jury will award judgment far in excess of the limits of the State Farm policy covering the Dilworths" and our firm conviction that "substantial punitive damages" would be included. We concluded that State Farm's failure to make reasonable settlement efforts would result in the company being held responsible for the entire amount of any judgment.

Our counterclaim simply set out the company's duty to provide Sheryl a defense under the terms of its policy issued to her, her father Eldon's standing as her administrator to collect what was due her, and a claim for our attorney fees in defending the action.

We also filed an objection to venue and a motion to transfer venue to Ford County, Kansas. Venue is a strange concept in the law. It generally includes one of several places in which a case may be filed and proceed to trial, usually, the place where facts giving rise to a cause of action occurred, where service of summons may be had on a necessary party, and where the witnesses are located. This motion was denied by Judge Rogg.

We next filed requests for discovery and notice to take the deposition of John Hoke. When the discovery requested was refused, we filed a motion to compel production. Our motion was denied by Judge Malone.

In the meantime, the original case in federal court was tried and a judgment, as predicted, rendered against the Dilworths. We moved to dismiss the state court action on the ground that any judgment of the state court would have no significance.

The court dismissed the action for lack of prosecution without notice to us, so it was necessary for us to have the action reinstated on the issue of our claim for attorney fees. Well, finally, we settled that issue upon an agreed payment of $10,000 to us.

It was simply amazing how these proceedings, one by one, came to naught without involving much forethought. It was certainly not typical of our friend Larry Withers, who, to his great credit, later convinced the company it should bond the judgment in order to pursue its appeal to the 10th Circuit.

ORAL ARGUMENT

The appeal was scheduled for oral argument on Monday, Nov. 18, 1991, at 9 a.m., so we elected to fly to Denver the afternoon before. It was a typically cold November day when we drove to the Wichita airport in Bradley's Ford conversion van. We parked along the curb just outside the United Airlines ticket counter to unload our bags and check in. We checked our bags through and headed for the restaurant area near the entrance to the gates.

After enjoying coffee and the usual upbeat conversation between "giant intellects," we headed to our assigned gate. We were early and so visited, discussed the case, and finally boarded. As experienced lawyers, having graduated and been admitted to practice in the 1950s, we felt confident and truly believed that we were right, that our brief was well-written, and that our clients' judgment would be upheld. We were ready with the also certain knowledge that our judgment would be fully paid because it was now fully bonded as elsewhere discussed. If successful, we also intended to pursue a claim for substantial fees against the "good neighbor," State Farm. We were soon to be reminded during the flight that we did sometimes, just sometimes, make mistakes and misjudgments, and sometimes were even overconfident-but weakness of intellect? Really now!

After flying an hour at 30,000 feet and beginning the long glide into the old Denver airport, we made an important discovery-Bradley reached into his pocket to discover NO KEYS TO THE VAN. We two great minds had left that big van, keys in the ignition, running, parked in the loading zone in front of United! When we arrived in Denver, a call home to ask Bradley's wife, Carolyn, to go move the van gained the response that the van had been confiscated, driven to a holding area, and could be reclaimed only by paying the appropriate storage and fines. Nothing like such an innocent oversight to bring two such now humble lawyers down to earth.

CAMPBELL V. STATE FARM

After hearing about and later reading the Utah case, Don and I agreed it was necessary to review in detail the amazing history of Campbell v. State Farm in order to present a better understanding of the events which happened in Sheryl's case. Campbell is a shortened reference to the case of Inez Preece Campbell and Matthew C. Barneck, Special Administrator and Personal Representative of the Estate of Curtis B. Campbell, plaintiff, v. State Farm Mutual Automobile Insurance Company, defendant, in the Supreme Court of the State of Utah, No. 981564, reported at 2004 UT 34, 98 P.3d 409 (April 23, 2004). The case cited is the finale of a series of court opinions using Campbell and State Farm on one side or the other of the caption. We also believed that if and when Campbell, possibly along with Sheryl's and other cases involving State Farm, fully broke into the news, State Farm might have to begin paying a price for its wrongdoing.

The Campbell case began in 1981 and the following narrative is from the opinion of the United States Supreme Court on a writ of certiorari issued to the Supreme Court of Utah.

"Curtis Campbell was driving with his wife, Inez Preece Campbell, in Cache County, Utah. He decided to pass six vans traveling ahead of them on a two-lane highway. Todd Ospital was driving a small car approaching from the opposite direction. To avoid a head-on collision with Campbell, who by then was driving on the wrong side of the highway and toward oncoming traffic, Ospital swerved onto the shoulder, lost control of his automobile, and collided with a vehicle driven by Robert G. Slusher. Ospital was killed, and Slusher was rendered permanently disabled. The Campbells escaped unscathed. State Farm Mut. Automobile Ins. Co. v. Campbell, 538 US 408 (April 7, 2003)."

Slusher and heirs of Ospital filed suit in the Utah state court to recover damages for the personal injuries of Slusher and the wrongful death of Ospital. Campbell, who was the defendant in that action, was insured by State Farm Mutual Insurance Company (hereafter "State Farm") under a policy with limits of liability of $50,000. Despite the offer of the plaintiffs to accept the payment of $25,000 each in full settlement, State Farm took the case to trial, against the advice of its own investigators. State Farm assured the Campbells that their assets were safe and that they had no liability for the accident and that they did not need their own attorney, that State Farm would represent their interests.

A JURY FOUND CAMPBELL 100% AT FAULT AND RETURNED A VERDICT FOR $185,849.

State Farm at first refused to cover the $135,849 excess (above the policy limits) and its counsel made the matter forcefully clear to the Campbells suggesting, "You may want to put 'for sale' signs on your property to get things moving." In other words, the Campbells were told they, not State Farm, would be responsible for this huge shortfall of coverage.

State Farm also refused to post a supersedeas bond for Campbell to stay collection of the judgment and allow him to appeal the decision.

Faced with this alarming and unexpected situation, Slusher, Ospital, and the Campbells agreed to join forces against what had now become their common enemy, State Farm.

Under this agreement, the attorneys representing Slusher and Ospital agreed to pursue a bad faith action for the Campbells against State Farm. The division of any verdict was to go 90% to Slusher and Ospital, who would have the right to play a part in all major decisions concerning the bad faith action and prior approval of any settlement. In 1989, on Campbell's appeal of the original judgment, the Utah supreme court refused any relief, whereupon State Farm paid the entire judgment, including the excess above its $50,000 policy limits.

In pursuit of their agreement reached in the meantime, the

Campbells filed suit against State Farm alleging bad faith, fraud, and intentional infliction of emotional distress. These grounds for suit will be explained later.

On first consideration, the Utah state court granted judgment to State Farm because it had paid the excess verdict. This ruling resulted in another appeal, and in a 1992 decision reported at 840 P.2d 130 (Utah App. 1992), the Utah supreme court reversed the lower court, reinstating the suit as originally filed.

When the case was sent back to the lower court, State Farm filed a motion asking the judge to exclude any evidence of its conduct in other cases or claims outside Utah. The judge denied this motion and State Farm, apparently as an alternative solution, asked the court to split the case and try it in two phases to two separate juries. The first phase was to determine only the issue of whether it was unreasonable for State Farm to refuse to settle with Slusher and Ospital rather than risk trial. This jury found that State Farm's decision was unreasonable because there was a substantial likelihood of a verdict in excess of the $50,000 policy limits, which proved to be the case, as we have seen.

The second phase was to determine State Farm's liability for fraud and intentional infliction of emotional distress, as well as to determine the amount of damages to be allowed to compensate the Campbells for these two elements of injury.

The Utah supreme court characterized this phase of the trial in the following terms: State Farm argued during phase II that its decision to take the case to trial was an "honest mistake" that did not warrant punitive damages. In contrast, the Campbells introduced evidence that State Farm's decision to take the case to trial was a result of a national scheme to meet corporate fiscal goals by capping payouts on claims company wide. This scheme was referred to as State Farm's "Performance, Planning and Review," or PP&R, policy. To prove the existence of this scheme, the trial court allowed the Campbells to introduce extensive expert testimony regarding fraudulent practices *by State Farm in its nation-wide operations. Although State Farm moved prior to phase II of the trial for the exclusion of such evidence and continued to object to it at trial, the trial court ruled that such evidence was admissible to determine whether State Farm's conduct in the Campbell case was indeed intentional and sufficiently egregious to warrant punitive damages. Campbell v. State Farm, 65 P.3d 1134 at 1143, 2001 WL 1245575, at *3 (Campbell I).*

Whatever options were open to State Farm at this point to head off the disastrous effects of the exposure of its grossly unfair and fraudulent practices nationwide were now shut with a bang.

This ruling and what followed serves to illustrate the importance to our system of justice when brilliant, aggressive, and resourceful trial lawyers expose for the benefit of the entire nation the hidden deceit and systematic corruption of State Farm's claims section in the interest only of amassing great wealth, to the great injury of its agents and policyholders. What the final results could be remain to be seen.

So much has been said and written about greedy, irresponsible lawyers filing groundless claims that this little vindication seems needful.

We will enumerate hereafter in detail some of the court's findings, but first the results of the second phase. The jury awarded the Campbells $2.6 million in compensatory and $145 million in punitive damages. The trial court reduced these awards to $1 million and $25 million, respectively. Both parties appealed.

The U.S. Supreme Court reversed the trial court's judgment, in effect saying that the $25 million punitive damages was a denial of due process, in violation of the 14th Amendment to the United States Constitution, leaving for the Utah supreme court to resolve the amount of punitive damages. In a carefully thought out, expressive opinion, the Utah Supreme Court concluded that $9,018,780.75, an amount nine times greater than the amount of compensatory and special damages, should be allowed.

Most instructive and revealing of all the opinions rendered was that of the Honorable William B. Bohling, Utah trial court judge, whose findings of fact on Phase II of the bifurcated trial are undisturbed. After 29 days of trial and extended consideration of the evidence, the court, in an excellent 74-page opinion, made known his observations on State Farm's conduct, including the following points:

1. State Farm's official policy was giving its adjusters undisclosed incentives to deny consumers benefits owed them in order to enhance profits by wrongfully turning its claims handling process into a profit center.

2. State Farm used various wrongful means to conceal this profit scheme and evade punishment for it.

3. It gave its claim adjusters specific numerical targets with regard to average payouts per claim.

4. Meeting these targets led to better pay and promotional prospects; missing them led to criticism, retarded prospects, and ultimately threatened employment.

5. The "Performance, Planning, and Review" program, or PP&R program, was covered in a 1979 document-since destroyed by the company-and was a comprehensive program for turning claims into an unjust department for unjust profits.

6. The arbitrary payment goals were set to apply to claims that had not yet happened.

7. Adjusters were instructed to "list prior damage to cars involved in accidents" in order to reduce the cost of repairs allowed.

8. "Negotiate appearance allowances" was again an unfair factor to reduce the amount paid.

9. Adjusters were referred to as the "big spenders" whose responsibility was to "shore up the bottom line," i.e., pay less than fairness demands.

10. The goal was to ensure that State Farm has the "most profitable claim service in the industry."

11. Expert testimony labeled these practices as "inherently wrong," could not be justified in any way, violated "the duty to treat insureds honestly and fairly," simply taboo in the insurance industry, absolutely wrong, "just absolutely what you would never want to see in a claims organization," creating a corporate culture that is predatory and takes advantage of gullible and defenseless people.

12. The PP&R program applied equally to the handling of both third-party and first-party claims.

13. The PP&R program applied to the lowest adjuster and went up through the ranks of management.

14. When one 30-year employee went to top managers, he was told to "get out of the kitchen" if he could not stand the heat. The "heat" in this case was personal dishonesty.

15. Another complaining employee was advised to be "more of a team player." She ultimately resigned.

16. The plan was not local, but a nationwide feature of State Farm's business operations, orchestrated at the highest levels.

17. To avoid detection, written accounts of this policy were destroyed and carried on only verbally.

18. Evidence was falsified in claim files. For example, in Ospital's file was the note he was speeding to get to his pregnant girlfriend's house, untrue on both counts.

19. Evidence was withheld in claim files for the same fraudulent purpose.

20. For the past two decades, State Farm has resorted to a variety of wrongful means to attempt to evade detection of and liability for its unlawful profit scheme, persuaded that:

a) few victims realize they are wronged,

b) fewer still will be able to sue,

c) only a small fraction will be able to weather the years of litigation to reach trial, and

d) few will be allowed punitive damages against the claim of "honest mistake" and a body of evidence it has systematically sanitized, padded, purged, concealed, destroyed, or rehearsed.

21. State Farm has relied on five principal evasion tactics:

a) systematic targeting of vulnerable and defenseless consumers, "the weakest of the herd," elderly, poor, least knowledgeable;

b) systematic destruction of documents requested in litigation that reveal the profit scheme,

c) destroying unfavorable corporate memory, and

d) replacing it with favorable versions,

e) retrieving unfavorable documents from previous claims litigation.

22. Failing to inform officials of punitive damage awards in order to allow them to claim innocence and ignorance of such claims or "honest mistake."

23. Adding self-serving statements in claim files.

24. Systematic manipulation of testimony by employees (coaching, creating memory).

25. Systematic efforts to intimidate claimants, witnesses, and attorneys, asking personal questions, such as indebtedness, infidelity, personal relationships.

26. Making litigation as time-consuming, expensive, and prolonged as possible for "in terrorem" value, sometimes referred to by State Farm consultants as "mad dog defense tactics."

Campbell v. State Farm, August 3, 1998, Court's Findings, Conclusions and Order Regarding Punitive Damages and Evidentiary Rulings (Trial Judge William B. Bohling). Many extensions and variations on these items and some direct testimony of former employees and experts could be added, but these items should suffice to warn people of the past and/or present danger of having done long-term business with State Farm.

As a final reminder, we cite the following from the U.S. Supreme Court's assessment of State Farm's overall profit scheme:

> *State Farm's "policies and practices," the trial evidence thus bore out, were "responsible for the injuries suffered by the Campbells," and the means used to implement those policies could be found "callous, clandestine, fraudulent, and dishonest"* (finding "ample evidence" that State Farm's reprehensible corporate policies were responsible for injuring "many other Utah consumers during the past two decades"). *The Utah Supreme Court, relying on the trial court's record-based recitations, understandably characterized State Farm's behavior as "egregious and malicious." State Farm Mut. Automobile Ins. Co. v. Campbell, 538 U.S. 408 (2003), at 436 [citations omitted].*

State Farm v. Schlossberg

Donald Shultz noted and brought to our attention yet another important case with a series of opinions involving State Farm concerning the wrongful death of a 15-year-old boy and an injured passenger on July 12, 1980, and tried in the circuit court for Prince George's County, Maryland, in 1982. Assessed damages resulted in a verdict of $1,163,534.36, later reduced to $502,412.11. The insurance limits for Watkins were $20,000 and Larson were $50,000, respectively. Offers for settlement had been made but were refused by State Farm. Also, State Farm refused to provide a copy of its "Excess Liability Handbook," copies of its manuals and copies of its videotapes. This resulted in a default judgment against State Farm. State Farm Mut. Auto. Ins. Co. v. Schlossberg, 570 A.2d 328, 82 Md.App. 45 (March 1, 1990). The fact that the Campbell case occurred in Utah, the Bergeson case in Kansas, and the Schlossberg case in Maryland seemed to support the claim that State Farm's illicit conduct had a nationwide pattern.

State Farm's PP&R Program

The PP&R program was a scheme designed and instituted to further enrich State Farm by turning its claim-handling department into a profit center. The means by which the highest company officials hoped to accomplish this seemingly impossible goal was to prey upon the most weak and most vulnerable who might have valid first- and/or third-party claims against the company. The company's tactic to settle such claims for less than fair value was even to be used against other State Farm policyholders in two-vehicle accidents. Adjusters and other claims handling employees were to be compensated in part for using unlawful or unethical practices to save money or to deny claims.

It was in 1979 when the excess liability and other handbooks were replaced by the document containing the outrageous PP&R program. (Our efforts to obtain an actual copy of that program were unsuccessful, but the Utah and United States Supreme Court decisions both carefully described it.)

At the top of the list for duplicitous conduct of State Farm toward the Dilworths was its attempt to shift all liability for punitive damages to them, even before the case was tried or punitive damages assessed.

As soon as plaintiff's motion to amend was granted and claims were amended to include punitive damages, the issue of who would have to pay them was of great concern to State Farm. It contacted multiple claim superintendents and superiors, along with lawyers and researchers in Texas [where the Dilworths' policy was written], in Kansas [where the collision occurred], and in Bloomington, Illinois [where its home offices are located]. These officials and researchers concluded in their November 15, 1989, seven-page claim report that State Farm would be responsible for both compensatory and punitive damages up to the $200,000 limits of its policy with the Dilworths. (We have no way of knowing the full extent of their conclusions because the copy we received was an "edited copy," with sections redacted.) At no time did State Farm advise the Dilworths or Sheryl's attorneys of that conclusion. Despite the unanimous conclusion of its claims supervisors and lawyers, it specifically denied the Dilworths coverage for any punitive damages. In its subsequent December 1, 1989, letter from John Hoke to Edward K. Dilworth, State Farm stated:

> Accordingly, protection will not be afforded by this policy of insurance for any punitive damages accessed against you. Therefore, we categorically deny coverage to you and anyone claiming coverage under your policy for any judgment for punitive damages.

It also sued the Dilworths and Sheryl's parents in Kansas state court for declaratory judgment seeking denial of punitive coverage under its policy. State Farm never raised its settlement offer of $65,000, but because of the claim for punitive damages, did internally raise its assessment of the claim value (including punitive) to $125,000, which was never offered. To the contrary, State Farm stood on its denial and told the Dilworths in no uncertain terms that it was specifically denying any and all liability for punitive damages.

Because of the fiduciary relationship State Farm owed the Dilworths, we believed its failure to reveal material facts concerning policy coverage for punitive damages after being forced to bond the entire judgment constituted a continuing fraud. It also constituted fraud for State Farm to make settlement offers only up to its evaluation of $65,000 for compensatory damages, rather than its later evaluation of $125,000 which included potential punitive damages. State Farm stood on its $65,000 offer even though Judge Theis, after hearing the evidence, opined that it was a mistake not to have offered the policy limits, even before the jury returned its verdict.

In the previous discussion of Campbell I (the 2001 Utah supreme court decision), many of the items of wrongful conduct set out by the trial court have obvious application to the Bergeson case.

Item 1: The PP&R program to turn claims handling into a profit center and to pay bonuses for saving the company money would have been in effect. (We have no specific documents to prove this fact and such documents, including the 1979 manual, were undoubtedly destroyed during the destruction program put in place in 1988 and thereafter.)

Undoubtedly *Item 13*, applying to adjusters up through the ranks, was in force. John Hoke, a leading claim superintendent and one of those in charge of the Bergeson file, wrote specifically that punitive damages were covered in the case, yet to be a "company man" he was also instructed to write the letter to the Dilworths denying any coverage for punitive damages.

It would appear that *Item 15*, discussing employees being "more of a team player," or possibly *Item 14*, when some of the adjusters were told to "get out of the kitchen if they couldn't stand the heat," may have had application. Certainly *Items 18 and 19* would apply: withholding evidence in claim files for fraudulent purposes. This occurred repeatedly during discovery and on one occasion caused State Farm counsel to apologize because they had not provided claim files to him which he should have received and later provided to us pursuant to court order.

Item 21 was obviously in force in this case: The targeting of vulnerable consumers and, in this case, policyholders. Undoubtedly the fact that it would be so difficult and agonizing for the parents of a wonderful young daughter to go through an actual trial replaying the wrongful death and physical injuries was probably one of the factors in State Farm's making a low-ball settlement offer and standing on it before, during, and even after the trial.

Item 23: adding self-serving statements in claim files. The Bergeson claim is absolutely littered with such statements throughout the file in an effort to show that it was not guilty of bad faith or fraud if a later lawsuit were filed. In fact, it had the following comment in one of its Claim Committee reports: *The aforementioned is to recap our handling and that we have, at all times, acted in good faith and have not gone against the wishes of the insureds' personal attorney. It was the considered opinion of all interested parties that the death claim had maximum value of $65,000.*

Item 26: making litigation as time-consuming, expensive, and prolonged as possible. Sometimes referred to by State Farm consultants as "mad dog" defense tactics, they were certainly in full force and effect. Litigation in Sheryl's case covered a period of approximately 9 years, before several courts, in various locales and jurisdictions. Various motions and delaying tactics were used, and State Farm actually went so far as to sue both the Dilworth policyholders and Sheryl's parents in state court seeking to have the policy construed as to punitive damages, even though no judgment had been obtained. After numerous proceedings in the state court case, it was finally dismissed, and plaintiff's lawyers were paid $10,000 for their expenses for this additional time-consuming proceeding against State Farm.

THE RECKONING

Despite the fact that the primary concern of Eldon and Marearl, Sheryl's parents, was not the recovery of money, but only as it reflected her vindication from her cruel death and the lies the Dilworths told about its true cause, we felt her story would not be complete without a reckoning of what it cost State Farm Mutual Automobile Insurance Company. The following is a chronological account.

On May 11, 1992, the Clerk of the United States District Court for the District of Kansas, pursuant to order dated May 8, 1992, paid to Donald E. Shultz the amount of $887,424.53, covering the judgment, including interest at 8.32%, in full payment of the judgment entered against the Dilworths. This included court costs of $915.68.

On May 8, 1992, State Farm paid additional court costs imposed by the 10th Circuit Court of Appeals, payable to Eldon Bergeson, in the amount of $584.14.

On May 12, 1992, State Farm paid to Bradley Post and Donald E. Shultz the amount of $10,000.

On March 20, 1995, the court clerk made payment to Shultz & Associates, in trust for the plaintiffs, the amount of $159,216.56, in attorney fees to reimburse plaintiff for his attorney fees in pursuing the garnishment.

RECAPITULATION:

5-08-92 JUDGMENT, COST, AND INTEREST...... $887,424.53

ADDITIONAL COSTS IMPOSED BY THE COURT OF APPEALS $584.14

5-12-92 BRADLEY POST & DONALD E. SHULTZ, ATTORNEY FEES FOR DEFENSE OF DECLARATORY JUDGMENT ACTION $10,000.00

3-20-95 DONALD E. SHULTZ, AS TRUSTEE FOR PLAINTIFFS, REIMBURSEMENT TO PLAINTIFFS FOR ATTORNEY FEES IN GARNISHMENT PROCEEDINGS $159,216.56

TOTAL AMOUNT PAID BY STATE FARM $1,057,225.23

We have no record of attorney fees and expenses paid to defense attorneys or their witnesses, Mr. Ames, or others.

The amount shown above was paid for a case State Farm evaluated at $65,000 for the death claim and not more than $75,000 for punitive damages. The claim superintendent suggested an offer of $125,000 be offered before trial. The $125,000 was never offered.

Was Sheryl vindicated? No, only as it indicated a verification of her innocence and the culpability of the Dilworths and their unnamed partner at trial, State Farm.

THE PIP FILE

In reviewing the content of State Farm records coming into our custody by Bradley's discovery sweep, we came across one called, "PIP file - Bergeson v. Dilworth." The principal topic of this file covered insurance required by Kansas law, which mandated certain required coverage for every person owning and registering an automobile. PIP stands for "personal injury protection."

The file reflects that State Farm, under Sheryl's policy, paid Eldon and Marearl, her parents, $2,731.50 death and hospital benefits, which would have been due, at least in part, under the liability policy covering the Dilworths. Under the same claim number, they paid off the balance due Chrysler Credit in Denver on Sheryl's Colt. The company paid her parents $439.09 for the equity Sheryl had in the car.

The company was critical of the attorney's handling of the PIP claim, assuming that was the purpose for which attorneys were employed. While we cooperated with the company, we did not enter into the tedium of deciding which losses were assigned to which policies. Our concern was that the Dilworths' liability file should bear the responsibility for all the loss, including what would, in the absence of their fault, be covered under Sheryl's PIP coverage. Even though the amounts were not that great, it seems unfair that any part of our claim should be reduced by insurance Sheryl had purchased.

In the verdict, the funeral and medical expenses were allowed, but we failed to ask for the loss of the automobile. State Farm never suggested that it was entitled to any credit for the amounts paid under Sheryl's PIP coverage and, probably, no credits would have been proper, but we also might have made them pay twice for the vehicle.

Our pursuit, however, was the larger claim: the pain and suffering to Sheryl and the loss to her parents from her death. Sometimes in pursuit of the bear, the hunter overlooks the rabbit.

Settlement Negotiations

From the time of our initial employment and even after the verdict, we pursued diligent efforts to settle this case. The contract called for a contingent fee of 33 1/3% on settlement, which increased to 40% if a lawsuit were filed, and 50% if appealed. If the claim could be fairly settled, it was our responsibility and to the client's benefit to do so.

Much depends on the valuation placed on a claim by the insurer, its claims people and, particularly, its attorneys. It is difficult to determine whose suggestions ruled in the valuations placed on this claim which caused it to be so lightly regarded. Here you have, on one hand, a lovely, exemplary young woman at the threshold of her career and, on the other, two careless, cruel, and indifferent parties who caused her death by conduct amounting to negligent homicide and the report of an expert accident reconstructionist placing the blame squarely on those insureds. These factors are simply omitted or were not discussed in the reports of the claims committee.

The settlement negotiations began with a lower-level regional claims office in Garden City with an offer of $25,000, intended to create the impression that their insureds had low limits of coverage. From the outset, knowing that the claim, even apart from any punitive damages, should far exceed $25,000, we steadfastly refused any settlement proposals unless and until we were told the limits of liability under the Dilworths' policy.

Other efforts to settle before trial are discussed in the section covering the claim committee report. In the conclusion of that report, it is stated that neither defense counsel (Mr. Warta nor Mr. Withers) placed a value on the death claim in excess of $65,000.

This may indicate that the claims people set this value and counsel simply went along with their suggestion, or much more likely, did not object. If this was the case, the reasons counsel would not dispute this should be obvious.

After the judgment was entered, it was not left up to State Farm to decide what to do. Bradley immediately proceeded to attempt collection of the judgment by a legal proceeding called "garnishment in aid of execution." "Execution" is the legal term used for collecting a judgment. "Garnishment" is the process of making a party who owes a duty to the defendant to pay the judgment or someone who simply owes a debt or holds property belonging to the judgment debtors. In this case, the Dilworths were the judgment debtors and State Farm, by virtue of its policy of indemnity insurance, owed them the duty to pay not only the $200,000 provided by their policy, but any excess because the Dilworths had insisted State Farm settle for that amount and State Farm chose, at its peril, to go it alone. The claim committee met again.

THE JOHN HOKE FILE

Part of the discovered items was the file of John Hoke, claim superintendent for State Farm. It contains a series of statements for services rendered from Foulston Siefkin, the fine firm with which Mr. Warta is associated. Each statement was accompanied with a cover letter in precisely the same language.

Dear John:

Enclosed is our interim statement for services rendered and monies advanced in the above-captioned matter. I trust you will find our statement satisfactory, but if you have any questions, please don't hesitate to contact me.

The first file included billings from January 15, 1988, to April 12, 1990. However, the copies of the checks issued are 20 in number while the billings number only 12. Obviously, we are missing part of the file, which might be explained by the fact that any confidential communications could safely have been excluded under the attorney-client confidential exception to items which are subject to discovery. The statements themselves are interesting, in their contrast to our billing practice for clients who were not under a contingent fee contract. In our billings, we describe the date and the services performed, together with a notation of the time spent in performing such services. Each amount of time was then multiplied by the hourly rate charged by the person performing those services itemized, then totalled at the end. Different attorneys' hourly rates varied and clerical services by legal assistants were charged at a much lower rate, and all this was reflected on the billing.

There is no indication that John Hoke or anyone else questioned this practice.

WINDING DOWN OF THE BANKRUPTCY

We left the bankruptcy with both the debtors and State Farm filing appeals from the order lifting the stay for Eldon Bergeson. Thereafter, the debtors (the Dilworths) filed a motion to lift the stay on their behalf, as previously described. This motion was later amended. On hearing, this motion was denied, and, again, Dilworths and State Farm appealed.

On an appeal, certain procedural requirements have to be met. The more important of these were not met and the appeals in both matters were simply dismissed by the court.

Once the appeal from the judgment in the federal district court in Kansas was bonded, so that State Farm became responsible to pay unless the case was reversed, the Dilworths' bankruptcy wound down.

On May 13, 1992, we filed our Notice of Withdrawal of Creditor's Dischargeability Complaint Under Section 523(1)(6) in each debtor's case, setting out as our reasons: 1) Senior United States District Court Judge for the District of Kansas, Frank G. Theis, had issued an order finding that he had exclusive jurisdiction of the subject matter of the supersedeas bond and all necessary parties and he had authorized and directed the clerk to pay out such funds to the creditor Eldon Bergeson on the 8th day of May, 1992; 2) Creditor's claim based upon a tort judgment against defendant (Dilworth) has been satisfied in full, pursuant to a supersedeas bond; and 3) The issue as to creditor's dischargeability complaint . . . is, therefore, moot and should be removed from the docket. Thereafter, the Dilworths were granted a discharge from their other debts and their bankruptcy was closed.

The Claim Committee

While the lawyers for Sheryl's parents were about their work, State Farm had its own strategy proceedings in place through a committee of its claims people, to which reference has been previously made. The committee members were John Hoke, claim superintendent, and Mendell F. Butler, state claim superintendent, and a number of other claims people at different levels having a continuous interest in the evaluation of this claim by the claim committee.

The first report in the file is on a printed form prepared for that purpose in which the various stages of thinking are addressed. In Re-Hearing 1, "settlement value other than no fault" and "settlement value other than no fault dated March 9, 1987," were to be considered. The policy limits and reserves were listed, the most recent being $50,000, and the first, merely $2,320 set on September 16, 1986, just 12 days after Sheryl's death. Under "additional remarks," is this note:

Since the previous claim committee, we have made a settlement offer in the amount of $35,000 and received an initial demand of $275,000. We refused to divulge the policy limits, but the plaintiff's attorney has concluded that they are above $100,000, and, thus, has offered to settle for over policy limits.

Under the "advisory" section, the report concluded:

Death claim of Bergeson has maximum value of $65,000. Structured settlement should be explored at $45,000.

This decision was reached on August 19, 1987.

On the reverse side of the report was a comparative evaluation of both plaintiff's and State Farm's attorneys. The reported opinion of their attorneys was that "the claim does not have the value of our policy limits." The recommendation of their claim representative Scott Miller was to settle up to $60,000. With this recommendation, John Hoke agreed.

Under a category entitled "coverage questions," John Hoke reached certain conclusions on the attorneys' legal basis for evaluating the claim, particularly with regard to the Wentling case, which Bradley tried, resulting in a verdict of $786,166.64. He followed with an argument distinguishing the two cases factually. The warning that it contained that Bradley was capable of obtaining verdicts far in excess of what anyone but he expected was missed by Mr. Hoke.

The report concludes: *The plaintiff has reminded us in his recent demand letter of our duty to the insured and has attempted to set us up in the event we refused to settle for the policy limits that he has demanded. We do not see our exposure anywhere near policy limits.*

Note the ominous sound attached to those words underlined-"to set us up." A second warning sounded but was ignored.

It does not appear that anyone on the claim committee ever bothered at this point to compare the two parties or their relative culpability or innocence, and project for trial purposes a likely outcome.

SECOND REHEARING

In its further rehearing, the claim committee refers to the statement taken from Theodora Koslowski and the narrow escape she experienced in meeting the weaving trailer pulled by Nathan Dilworth. Also referenced is a letter Sheryl's mother wrote to the Wichita Eagle urging new and stronger laws concerning the movement of construction equipment on Kansas highways, pointing out the inadequate brakes and the Dilworth trailer as examples. Mr. Hoke discussed this with the defense attorney, who advised that this "would be used to demonstrate an uncaring attitude of the defendant and that would be their basis to request punitive damages."

Mention was made of a letter to Bradley from the Dilworths indicating that Sheryl was "either asleep, putting cassette tapes in to play, or was trying to commit suicide." The report reckoned if this letter got to the jury it might inflame them and could well add to the punitive damage award. Note the underlined portion above. "Add to" suggests that the attorney had suggested punitive damages as a probability.

The Dilworths at one point demanded that State Farm file a counterclaim, but Darrell Warta, to his credit, refused to do so.

Under "coverage questions," the superintendent's opinion was that, because the policy was issued in Texas where punitive damages are presumed to be covered by the policy, it would likewise extend the same benefits to an accident occurring in Kansas. To his credit at this point, he suggested increasing the offer to $125,000 or proceed to trial.

Also mentioned early in this report was the Dilworth demand that State Farm pay policy limits or accept responsibility for any excess judgment above policy limits. Still, to this point, there was no careful analysis by anyone, of the qualities of this young woman, now dead, or the dimensions of culpability of their insureds and their want of any offsetting virtues.

This report also includes reference to a declaratory judgment action filed in the state court in Sedgwick County, as follows:

It is obvious the plaintiff attorney's position is to stall any declaratory judgment action until the verdict is obtained. It seems logical that a district court trial judge might well follow that logic, in that if there were no punitive damages awarded then the declaratory action would be a moot issue.

REHEARING NUMBER 3

This report raised the company's reserve to $200,000 and reported on the verdict rendered on May 3, 1990, awarding a total of $906,795.33, which was reduced (because of the legislative cap on non-pecuniary loss[1]) to $756,795.33. It was State Farm's decision that the entire decision be appealed to the 10th Circuit while tendering their $200,000, plus interest.

[1]The limit could not be revealed to the jury–a fact we hope will be changed on the basis of fairness or jury reasoning.

Excess Judgment

The history of State Farm in relation to its dealings with its insureds, the Dilworths, was next discussed in relation to the responsibility for any judgment in excess of the coverage limits.

We continue to keep the defendants [Dilworths] advised of plaintiff's demands, our evaluation, and suggested the defendant employ personal counsel. This was, in fact, done by the defendants Dilworth, with employment of Wayne B. Ames, attorney at law, Allen, Texas.

The day before the trial was to commence, Mendell Butler, Darrell Warta, and Mr. Ames met to review various aspects of the case and Ames "was in complete agreement" with the value of $65,000 which they put on the death claim and the limited exposure on punitive damages. Although the claim committee had earlier rated the plaintiff's lawyers and their own lawyer, no effort was here made to rate the skill or experience of this lawyer whose agreement they sought in an effort to avoid sole responsibility for the excess.

The next paragraph of the report must be repeated in full in order that its self-serving, we may say "backside-covering," nature may be fully comprehended.

The aforementioned is to recap our handling and that we have, at all times, acted in good faith and have not gone against the wishes of the insureds' personal attorney. It was the considered opinion of all interested parties that the death claim had maximum value of $65,000. The results of the trial were totally unexpected, were not anticipated, and appear to have resulted from the jury being totally infuriated by the defendants and various documents written by defendant Edward Dilworth to plaintiff's attorney, Bradley Post (see page 2 of attorney Warta's May 9, 1990, letter). The letters in question should not have gone, however, the court so allowed.

Reference is then made to a letter from Mr. Warta dated May 9, 1990, in which he attempts to explain what happened that resulted in such a large departure from their estimates, recommending an appeal to the 10th Circuit without filing a motion for a new trial which he regarded as "an exercise in futility."

He knew Judge Theis's comments about the case and the policy limits, which were in obvious conflict with State Farm's evaluations.

State Farm still believed it had no exposure at all for punitive damages and only $56,795.33, the excess of actual or claimed damages above their policy limits. They obviously felt that an appeal of the judgment would force Bradley into a position to consider a compromise settlement, made mention of the garnishment action, and put forward the notion that paying their $200,000 into court would stop the running of interest on the $756,795.33 judgment. The report offers no source for these conclusions. Reference is made to the case of Guaranty Abstract v. Interstate Fire & Casualty Company, a copy of which was attached, one of a series of cases dealing with responsibility for excess judgments.

The report concludes:

In the interim, it is recommended that we proceed with the appeal to the 10th Circuit Court in Denver and thereafter be guided by events and recommendations of attorney Withers and attorney Bowman as to their representations of State Farm on the excess exposure. Once again, in keeping with its protective guidelines, State Farm felt it was necessary to include comments claiming to be guided by its attorneys on the excess judgment issues.

Might She Have Been Spared?

What might have spared Sheryl's life? What laws or what measures might have kept her young blessing among us?

What consideration should be given to the moral risk in selling liability insurance? Considering what this claim ultimately cost State Farm, would it not have been wise to inquire into the people they were insuring and the equipment, at least in the form of rolling stock, that was being used in their construction work? The most casual inspection would have revealed the added risk in the ball hitch with its stripped threads and the elongated hole in the bumper. How ugly does the profit motive here appear in the light of this lovely young lady's death?

Then there is the possible legislative protection. Suppose that a severe penalty were imposed for moving heavy equipment at night over highways without shoulders? The chance of detecting the faults in the Dilworth equipment would be very slight under the present random inspections. Only the presence of shoulders might have provided Sheryl a way of escape. And would any such law have altered the conduct of the Dilworths?

So the answer inevitably comes, "In a perfect world, Sheryl might have been spared." It was, nevertheless, fitting that State Farm, beguiled by the profit motive, should be compelled to pay, and pay, and pay they did.

THE WORD

Near the end of our work in Sheryl's case, we discovered some of the court opinions deciding the Campbell cases. In them, we noted the single word used by the appellate courts to determine how large a judgment in punitive damages could be justified and still be within legal guidelines to avoid being unconstitutionally large. One of the criteria used would be determined by the **"reprehensibility"** (the descriptive word) of the wrongful conduct justifying punitive damages and the amount thereof. The amount of the verdict carefully determined by the Campbell jury totaled $147.6 million: $2.6 million compensatory and $145 million punitive damages. The trial court reduced the damages to $1 million and $25 million, respectively, but the Utah supreme court reinstated the punitive damages (of $145 million). The U.S. Supreme Court remanded the case to the trial court, making it clear that the punitive award must be no larger than a single-digit in comparison to the compensatory award in order to comply with the 14th Amendment to be constitutional. Thus, the trial court finally set the amount of punitive damages at just over $9 million. This final punitive damage award was still nine times greater than the $1 million compensatory damages awarded.

We now invite readers of our book to judge whether the deceitful, wrongful conduct of State Farm Mutual Automobile Insurance Company in executing its PP&R program, as described in the Campbell opinions, along with its refusal to settle within the policy limits, was in fact "reprehensible" and, second, whether the PP&R program was applied and again vigorously executed in Sheryl's case against the Dilworths.

After hearing and reading about the *Campbell* decisions, Don and Bradley often discussed and wondered whether Mr. Ames or some other attorney for the Dilworths might file suit against State Farm for its failure to settle the case and failure to post the required appeal bond until forced to do so, causing extended litigation time and expense to all. To our knowledge no such litigation was ever pursued. It would have been interesting if the great Utah lawyers in *Campbell* could have somehow replaced Mr. Ames in a suit against State Farm for its reprehensible conduct against Sheryl, notwithstanding the terrible conduct of the Dilworths.

ADDENDUM

The preparation and jury trial of this case required great courage and willpower on the part of an upstanding Kansas family determined to set the record straight, despite the agony of participating in the preparation and trial of Sheryl Lynn's case.

As attorneys with the honor of representing Sheryl and her fine family, we feared the pain and distress they would suffer during the trial and in testifying before the Court and jury. For those reasons every effort was made to settle the case within insurance policy limits. Most contested cases can be settled without trial but some companies use personal tragedy or potential difficulty for opponents to justify attempts to save money with only low-ball settlement offers.

Some may wonder why Sheryl's case was not settled, so we are attaching copies of a few documents that concerned settlement attempts and responses. Of course defense counsel would have been controlled and directed by the cloud mentioned in the forward concerning settlement discussions. Even though differences arise during trials, we retain great respect for defense counsel and their law firms.

Post, Syrios & Bradshaw

Attorneys at Law
204 Occidental Plaza
300 North Main
Wichita, Kansas 67202-2078

Bradley Post
M. William Syrios
Arden J. Bradshaw

(316) 267-6391

August 6, 1987

Mr. John Hook, Claims Superintendent
State Farm Insurance Claim Office
401 Campus Drive, Suite 103
P. O. Box 1748
Garden City, Kansas 67846

Re: Your Insured: Edward Dilworth
Claim No.: 43-8126-574
D/O/L: 9-4-86
Our Client: Sheryl Bergeson

Dear Mr. Hook:

It is my understanding from our conversations that our settlement offer of $275,000 probably exceeds the liability policy limits of your insured, Edward Dilworth. It is also my belief, based on our conversation, that your company probably does have substantial coverage. In view of these facts, I am now authorized to submit for your consideration an offer to settle for an amount equal to your insured's policy limits. If this settlement can be made, we will be able to provide a full and complete release of liability for the tragic death of Sheryl Lynn Bergeson.

If settlement cannot be made at this time, we will proceed to file suit in the United States District Court and try the case. It is our view that we will probably obtain a judgment and that the judgment will likely exceed our compromise settlement demand, as well as your insured's policy limits. Because your offers have been so low, we will look to your company to pay the full amount of any excess above your policy limits unless Mr. Dilworth is able to pay. I am sure you are familiar with Kansas law regarding an insurer's duty in considering settlement proposals, but you might wish to take a look at Bollinger v. Nuss, 202 Kan. 326 (1969); Rector v. Husted, 214 Kan. 230 (1974); and Farmers Insurance Exchange v. Schropp, 222 Kan. 612 (1977).

I discussed with you during our recent telephone conversation the seminar on wrongful death held at the annual KBA meeting in Mr.

AUG 7 1987

John Hook, Claims Superintendent
August 6, 1987
Page 2

Wichita. One of your attorneys, Darrell Warta of Foulston, Siefkin, Powers & Eberhardt, was the moderator of that program. Much of the seminar was directed to the issue of damages in wrongful death actions and specifically, the opinion in Wentling v. Medical Anesthesia Services, P.A., 237 Kan. 503 (1985). I previously sent a copy of this opinion to Mr. Miller. Even though Mr. Warta is an extremely conservative defense lawyer, I would be very surprised if he reviewed this case and did not view our settlement offer of $275,000 to be reasonable and your offers to be unreasonably low.

Our offer will remain open for a period of at least 14 days before suit is filed, unless you should reject our offer sooner. Should you need additional time to consider our offer, please advise. If you have any questions or wish to discuss this case further, please contact me. An extra copy of this letter is included for your convenience in forwarding it to Mr. Dilworth for presentation to his personal attorney.

Yours very truly,

Bradley Post

Bradley Post

BP/rhw

cc: Mr. Donald Shultz

AUG 7 1987

September 11, 1987

Post, Syrios & Bradshaw
204 Occidental Plaza
300 North Main
Wichita, KS 67202-2078

Attention: Brandly Post

RE: Our Claim #: 43-8126-574
Our Insured: Edward K. Dilworth
Your Client: Sheryl Bergeson

Dear Mr. Post:

Please relay our offer of settlement to your clients. Our offer is in the amount of $65,000.00 to conclude the entire claim.

We would also like to offer a couple of structured settlement proposals and ask thattyou relay this to your clients.

The structured settlement proposals are as follows:

<u>First Proposal</u>: An immediate $15,000.00 up front payment with annual payments of $3,044.00 payable annually beginning November 1, 1987 for a period of 20 years. Total guaranteed payments equalling $75,880.00.

<u>Second Proposal</u>: An immediate $15,000.00 up front payment, plus monthly payments of $263.66 for a period of 20 years. Total guaranteed payments equalling $78,278.40.

If you are interested in the structured settlement proposals and desire some modification that could be accomplished as far as timing of payments, please let me know and we will try accommodate.

Sincerely yours,

John Hoke, CPCU
Claim Superintendent

JH/vrr

Post, Syrios & Bradshaw

Attorneys at Law
204 Occidental Plaza
300 North Main
Wichita, Kansas 67202-2078

Bradley Post
M. William Syrios
Arden J. Bradshaw

(316) 267-6391

September 30, 1987

Mr. John Hoke, CPCU
Claim Superintendent
State Farm Insurance Claim Office
Box 1748
Garden City, Kansas 67846

Re: Bergeson v. Dilworth

Dear Mr. Hoke:

This will acknowledge your letter of September 15, 1987, which included an offer to settle the above case. As I told you during our telephone conversation, that offer was submitted to our clients and it has now been rejected.

We are submitting, once again, our previous offer to settle for the policy limits. This offer is extended to the time the answer to the petition we are filing is due. If it has not been accepted before that time, it is withdrawn.

I am enclosing for your convenience and consideration a copy of the petition we are filing in federal court against your insured. If you have any questions or wish to discuss any matters concerning this petition, please feel free to contact Mr. Shultz or me.

Yours very truly,

Bradley Post

gh

Enclosures

cc: Mr. Donald E. Shultz

OCT 1 1987

Post, Syrios & Bradshaw

Attorneys at Law
204 Occidental Plaza
300 North Main
Wichita, Kansas 67202-2078

Bradley Post
M. William Syrios
Arden J. Bradshaw
Jeffrey L. Syrios

(316) 267-6391

December 8, 1988

Mr. Darrell L. Warta
Foulston Siefkin Powers & Eberhardt
Attorneys at Law
700 Fourth Financial Center
Wichita, Kansas 67202

Re: Bergeson v. Dilworth

Dear Darrell:

As you know, we have now concluded discovery in this case. I assume you will agree that a recovery against your clients for the wrongful death of Sheryl Bergeson is highly probable. This, of course, raises the question of the amount of damages the jury will award.

I have discussed the issue of damages with you on previous occasions. There is a sharp disagreement between the State Farm assessment of the probable jury verdict and my assessment. Recent cases I have tried involving the death of young women have resulted in verdicts in excess of $700,000 and $3 million. Nevertheless, we previously offered to settle this case with your clients for the amount of the State Farm policy limits. The response was the low-ball settlement offer of $65,000. This is even less than the statutory amount recoverable for bereavement alone.

I have recently reviewed a case from California which has wrongful death law almost identical to Kansas. In that case, DiRosario v. Havens, 196 Cal.App.3d 1224, 242 Cal.Rptr. 423 (1987), the total verdict rendered to the mother and father exceeded $2 million for a minor daughter who was struck by an automobile driver. An issue was raised as to whether there should have been a reduction in damages because of the necessity for the parents to support and educate the child. Obviously, that issue does not arise in our case since Sheryl had completed college.

Mr. Darrell Warta
December 8, 1988
Page 2

I think any reasonable person reviewing this case will have to agree that a verdict in the range of $1 million is a definite possibility and a verdict far in excess of the $200,000 coverage which State Farm claims is highly probable. It, therefore, seems to us that you are placing your insureds, the Dilworths, at risk for damages far in excess of the amount of their insurance coverage. As you know, Kansas law requires that an insurance company act in good faith and give the same consideration to the rights of its insureds as it does its own. It is obvious bad faith if State Farm does not offer its policy limits. It is also likely that State Farm would have to pay any excess verdict if the Dilworths demand that State Farm offer policy limits and its fails to do so.

Please send the extra copy of this letter and the DiRosario case to Edward and Nathan Dilworth so that they will be advised of our position and will have the opportunity to contact independent counsel and make demand on State Farm to immediately offer policy limits to avoid exposing them to the risk of damages far in excess of their liability coverage. As you know, the amount of the prayer in this case is $2 million. Should a judgment in excess of policy limits be obtained, we will be obligated to pursue the Dilworths with attachments, executions, and other remedies to recover any amount State Farm does not pay.

Yours very truly,

Bradley Post

gh

Enclosures

Post & Syrios

Attorneys at Law

204 Occidental Plaza · 300 North Main
Wichita Kansas 67202-2078

Bradley Post
M. William Syrios
Jeffrey L. Syrios

316-267-6391
Fax 316-267-7943

March 10, 1989

Mr. Darrell L. Warta
Foulston Siefkin Powers & Eberhardt
Attorneys at Law
700 Fourth Financial Center
Wichita, Kansas 67202

Re: Bergeson v. Dilworth

Dear Mr. Warta:

I have not been contacted by attorneys representing your clients Nathan and Edward Dilworth. I am therefore wondering whether you forwarded a copy of my December 8, 1988, letter and enclosures to them. I am sure you noted with interest the recent jury verdict of almost $160,000 reported in the Wichita paper for the wrongful death of a minor, 11 years old. I would request that this information be passed along to your clients so they can decide whether their personal attorney should be contacted to make demand upon State Farm. As I previously indicated to you, if trial results in a verdict in excess of the $200,000 policy limits, executions and all other legal remedies available will be pursued to collect the full amount of any judgment against your clients, regardless of the amount. Naturally, if your company is found to be in bad faith for failing and refusing to settle and pay this case when it had the opportunity, we would attempt to collect the full amount from State Farm.

I am enclosing an extra copy of this letter so this information can be made available to the Dilworths. As you know, this case is now set for trial on August 22, 1989, and we anticipate it will be tried at that time.

Yours very truly,

Bradley Post

Bradley Post

gh
Enclosure
cc: Mr. Donald E. Shultz

Post & Syrios
Attorneys at Law
204 Occidental Plaza - 300 North Main
Wichita, Kansas 67202-2078

Bradley Post
M. William Syrios
Jeffrey L. Syrios

(316) 267-6391
Fax (316) 267-7943

June 15, 1989

Mr. Darrell L. Warta
Foulston Siefkin Powers & Eberhardt
Attorneys at Law
700 Fourth Financial Center
Wichita, Kansas 67202

Re: Bergeson v. Dilworth and State Farm

Dear Mr. Warta:

I have recently discovered that a young man clearly identified as an insurance adjuster for State Farm Mutual Automobile Insurance Company took a recorded statement from Mrs. Harry Koslowsky, who is listed as a witness in this case. This man was representing State Farm when he took this statement. State Farm did not advise us as attorneys for the estate of Sheryl Bergeson, their insured, or her heirs that it was making secret investigations as an adversary in this pending litigation. Until I receive facts to the contrary, I will assume you had no knowledge of State Farm's adversarial conduct toward Sheryl's estate and her heirs contrary to the fiduciary relationship that exists between them. I will also assume that you did not receive a copy of this recorded statement and withhold it.

We demand that your client, State Farm, discontinue further breaches of its fiduciary duties which exist in matters related to this case. We request that any statements taken by insurance adjusters claiming to represent State Farm after suit was filed be immediately furnished to us with an explanation as to why they were taken and why they were kept secret. Naturally, I do intend to file a complaint with the state insurance commissioner and to take any other action necessary to prevent State Farm from choosing one side of the case where it has a clear conflict of interest. I also request that you immediately forward to me statements taken by State Farm not previously furnished and any memos or observations by any insurance adjusters or claims representatives concerning this case prepared after suit was filed.

It is my understanding that State Farm had a woman adjuster taking pictures at the scene within a day or two after this collision and

Mr. Darrell L. Warta
Page 2
June 15, 1989

I would appreciate it if you could identify her together with any other adjusters who have worked on this case.

Finally, please give me dates when you will be available within the next two weeks for depositions concerning these matters.

Yours very truly,

Bradley Post

gh

cc: Mr. Donald E. Shultz

FOULSTON, SIEFKIN, POWERS & EBERHARDT

LAW OFFICES

700 FOURTH FINANCIAL CENTER
BROADWAY AT DOUGLAS
WICHITA, KANSAS 67202
(316) 267-6371
FACSIMILE: (316) 267-6345

June 22, 1989

Bradley Post
POST & SYRIOS
204 Occidental Plaza
300 North Main
Wichita, Kansas 67202-2078

RE: Bergeson vs. Dilworth

Dear Brad:

I have your letters of June 12 and June 15, 1989.

In answer to the inquiry of your June 12th letter, my file reflects that I have sent a copy of your December 8, 1988, letter and its enclosures as well as a copy of your March 13th letter to the Dilworths at 610 Galbraith, Lake Dallas, Texas 75065. I have not heard from the Dilworths or any attorney that purports to represent their personal interest regarding that correspondence.

As for your letter of June 15, I don't understand your objection to the fact that I had an adjuster from State Farm take a recorded statement from Mrs. Harry Koslowsky.

For your information, I made it known to John Hoke, Claim Superintendent of State Farm, that the investigating officer had testified that he had talked with a Mrs. Koslowsky as part of his investigation and that Mrs. Koslowsky had told him that she had met a tractor-trailer on the highway shortly before the accident which gave rise to this lawsuit. Further, I advised him that the investigating officer testified that Mrs. Koslowsky had told him that the trailer had swayed across the centerline.

To: Bradley Post
Re: Bergeson vs. Dilworth
June 22, 1989
Page 2.

Accordingly, I requested that Mr. Hoke have an adjuster take a statement from Mrs. Koslowsky in an effort to clarify the investigating officer's testimony.

Such a statement was taken at my express direction.

Very truly yours,

Darrell L. Warta

of FOULSTON, SIEFKIN, POWERS & EBERHARDT

DLW/sfm

P.S. - Brad, this postscript is being added after our telephone conference of this morning. I have decided to share with you a copy of Ms. Koslowsky's statement which is enclosed.

bcc/enc: John Hoke, 43-8126-574
Edward and Nathan Dilworth

Post & Syrios
Attorneys at Law

204 Occidental Plaza · 300 North Main
Wichita, Kansas 67202-2078

Bradley Post
M. William Syrios
Jeffrey L. Syrios

(316) 267-6391
Fax (316) 267-7943

June 23, 1989

Mr. Darrell L. Warta
Foulston, Siefkin, Powers & Eberhardt
700 Fourth Financial Center
Wichita, Kansas 67202

Re: Bergeson v. Dilworth

Dear Darrell:

This will acknowledge receipt of your letter of June 22, 1989, and the statement obtained by the State Farm adjuster. Please send me any memos or reports by Mark Ptacek concerning this statement or Mrs. Koslowsky.

I also wish to put you on notice that when this case is tried we intend to seek punitive damages against the Dilworths for their gross and wanton negligence. We believe the evidence will establish that Mr. Dilworth knew or should have known that the trailer and backhoe were swaying across the center line, that this was dangerous to other people entitled to use the highways, and that he proceeded anyway. I believe the Dilworths should be furnished with a copy of Mrs. Koslowsky's statement.

As you know, punitive damages are not ordinarily covered by insurance in Kansas unless a company has acted in bad faith in its refusal to settle, and any punitive damages are not dischargeable in bankruptcy. Naturally, if punitive damages are levied in this case we will make every possible effort to pursue both the insurance company and the Dilworths personally to recover these damages. In our view, the compensatory damages alone far exceed the coverage under State Farm's policies.

An extra copy of this letter is enclosed and we request that it be forwarded to both Dilworths to see if they wish to retain their own counsel to represent their private interests in this matter. Naturally, if they do that we request that they instruct their counsel to contact us.

Yours very truly,

Bradley Post

gh/Enclosure

cc: Mr. Donald E. Shultz

FOULSTON, SIEFKIN, POWERS & EBERHARDT

LAW OFFICES

700 FOURTH FINANCIAL CENTER
BROADWAY AT DOUGLAS
WICHITA, KANSAS 67202
(316) 267-6371
FACSIMILE: (316) 267-6345

August 3, 1989

Bradley Post
POST & SYRIOS
204 Occidental Plaza
300 N. Main
Wichita, Kansas 67202-2078

RE: Bergeson vs. Dilworth

Dear Brad:

I want to clarify a statement that I made in the first page of my letter to you, dated June 22, 1989. In the second paragraph, I wrote, "I have not heard from the Dilworths or any attorney that purports to represent their personal interest regarding that correspondence."

I now know that on February 2, 1989, the Dilworths did write to claim superintendent, John Hoke of State Farm, regarding your letter of December 8, 1988. A copy of that letter has been provided to me.

Very truly yours,

Darrell L. Warta

of FOULSTON, SIEFKIN, POWERS & EBERHARDT

DLW/sfm

www.ingramcontent.com/pod-product-compliance
Lightning Source LLC
Chambersburg PA
CBHW021426170526
45164CB00001B/120

* 9 7 8 1 5 1 7 5 5 9 5 2 6 *